# Prais

"I found the book so ~~~~~~~~~~~
to give to my family and friends. Austin Harrison, former Boston
TV/Radio/Communications executive and PBS consultant.

"A wonderful collection. I'm reliving my last visit to Cannon Beach,
Oregon, and the fantastic creatures in the tide pools there." Suzanne
Wilson, Artist-in-Residence, nature and conservation author.

"I couldn't put it down. I read it straight through and really enjoyed it."
Jan Rife.

"A lovely book of poetry by an especially gifted poet. Inspiring and
impressive." B.J. Mitchell, Ph.D., Library Emeritus and author.

"I love Elliott Potter's drawings. I'm using the book as my inspiration
before I go to my sanctuary in the wee hours of the morn." Doris
Wardlow, author of *Legend of the Little Donkey, Gems from the Archives.*

"When I read *Elegy for Kay* and *Historic Homes Tour,* Kay became as real to
me as one of my friends. My love of flowers and *Addiction to the Rose* are
so much like the author's. Joe's favorites are *At the Piano* and all the water
and beach poems. We love the sketches, especially the sea oats." Marian
and Joseph E. Tienstra, M.D., Fellow, Am. College of Surgeons.

"(The book) just reaches out to me. How does she know how I feel?"
Eleanor Flanigan, past pres., *The Shakespeare Society,* founded 1887.

" The book is fantastic. I love it. When I read those coast, beach and surf
poems, I feel like I am right there in the scene, living it." Michelle
Naakens, equestrian, potter and rancher.

"Vivid word pictures which convey the music of the heart to the audience
of the mind." H.L. Thompson, Pastor Emeritus, author of *From the Heart.*

"A great book. My favorite is *For Elliott.*" Peggy O'Neill Aschermann,
champion athlete, author of *Clyde, A Letter from Heaven.*

# *By Surf and By Stream*

The author as a girl.

# Dedication

To everyone who helped me prepare this volume. You know who you are and what you have done.

To my husband Elliott Potter, always my first reader and greatest supporter, who illustrated this collection with his pen-and-ink drawings.

To my entire family of four generations, the best ever, beginning with my parents Perry and Lorraine Riley. My mother and my husband always said to me, "You can do anything you want to do." My late father also said it by his encouragement, the expression on his face and look of pride in his eyes.

Every single member of our family has helped me immensely in one way or another, from computer whizzes to designers, software and photography experts, book sellers and fellow writers, with critiques, many good ideas and suggestions.

To Jane Frieze Crawford, the tactful and patient editor of this collection, and to Sheila Tryk, who critiqued and edited "Spring River Saga" and contributed greatly to its layout. To Martha Curry, who also critiqued "Spring River Saga" and acted as final proof reader and copy editor in her invaluable way. Anna Rose Thomas, with her sharp young eyes and sharp young mind, saw so many things I had missed, and joined this illustrious group to critique and proofread. To Andrew Macklem-Cross for his advice.

And now to my children and grandchildren, I'm passing on the torch. Or should I say, pen? Or mouse?

# Contents

# Acknowledgments

I am grateful to my husband's parents Minford and Elizabeth Potter for their belief in me and also to former employers Roy Mayes, Sr. and Austin Harrison, who gave me work opportunities in which I learned many things.

I owe a great debt to all of the fine teachers, writers and speakers who have helped to guide me along the way, from my third grade teacher Miss Ackerman at P.S. 101 in Forest Hills, Long Island, N.Y., to English teacher Helen Minami at Woodrow Wilson Sr. High in Long Beach, Calif., Freshman English Instructor Wuliger at U.C.--Berkeley, Creative Writing Prof. Weireck at the Univ. of Ill., Champaign-Urbana, and many years later to Kay Kirkman, Creative Writing Instructor in Continuing Education at Mo. Southern State Univ., to Jean Hager, the Okla. novelist and speaker who helped me find my first agent, and at Okla. Univ., to Prof. Jack Bickham, director for many years of the Professional Writing Program and annual Short Course in Professional Writing at the H. H. Herbert School of Journalism and Prof. Emeritus Dwight V. Swain, author of the indispensable *Techniques of the Selling Writer*.*

Many colleagues, speakers and friends in writers' groups have been so ready to swap tips, critique and share knowledge of craft. I want to thank each one of you for your generosity and all you have taught me. Now I think especially of Frances Jones, Mary Bussinger, Suzanne Wilson, Dulcie Robertson, and Terry Zahniser McDermid.

*University of Oklahoma Press, Norman, Okla.

# *Preface*

All my life, the Muse of Poetry has visited me in nature, usually during solitary walks along the shore or by the creek where I live today. Sometimes the Muse brings fragments, phrases, lines, sometimes whole poems to later prune, refine and polish.

I need the earth, the sky, the weather, sun, moon and stars, trees, flowers, birds, and, if at all possible, water in any form, together with all the life in, along and around it. I need crashing waves, the tides, a lake, a spring, a rivulet, a tumbling stream moving quickly over rocks, the currents, shallows, depths and pools of a river, its bluffs and gravel bars.

I can walk outdoors by water anywhere in the world, but to welcome and listen to the Muse, I need solitude, away from the pressing crowds.

I need to take these quiet walks more often.

J.R.P.

## *Reason Enough for Me*

To feel both the heat of the sun
and the coolness of a gentle breeze
upon my skin–
to see the forms and colors
of all things with sharpness
through clear bright air–
to feel and to see
and then have the need to convey
the feeling and the seeing,
that is reason enough for being.

*La Fuente,* 1946, Long Beach, Calif.
*Islander,* May, 1974, Hilton Head, S.C.

# *Your Eyes*

Into those burning dark brown depths I dive
and revel long within your tender gaze.
What joy is brought by laughing eyes, alive
with bright pin points of light! How devious ways
in which we share a glance. Across the maze
of empty alien eyes, on winged feet
our mirth does rise, in eyes. Your glance allays
my pain. Shame, tears and anger all retreat,
as in your blessed dark brown eyes, our spirits meet.

*Islander,* November, 1973, Hilton Head Island, S.C.

## *Awakened at Dawn*

Under bare feet making their way to the beach,
the sand is delicious--soft, fine, neither warm nor cool.
Morning birds sing and call to one another
from their homes in the grassy dunes where
the sea oats grow.

Rose fire and golden light of sunrise break
through blue-gray thunderheads
disintegrating now and moving out to sea.
Wet sand and shallow oncoming waves

reflect rosy, golden light. A coconut palm
with gigantic roots and a double trunk rests on the
beach, stranded as high tide receded a while ago.
Snails work their trails in wet sand.

Each wave roars its way up the beach, mingling
its sound and form with the others.

I mingle my sound and form with others
of my kind as the waves do, for the waves
are part of the ocean and all waters on the earth.

I am one with all, a part of all. I'm only
another voice, only another form among billions,
and yet I am myself alone.

*Islander,* August, 1974, Hilton Head Island, S.C.

# May-June

Shaggy pink and white peonies shed their petals
to the earth. Late varieties of iris bloom and shrivel.
Roses open one by one in full May glory, then likewise
shatter. Graduates rejoice and party. Schools close to
the mutual satisfaction of teachers and students and
to secret dismay of parents. Memorial Day turns sedate
cemeteries into strange exotic seas of flower boxes and
gaudy plastic posies. Pools open. T-Ball and Little
League begin, and a ribbon of vacationers unfurls along
the Interstate. Early day lilies open wide with golden
light, and freshly planted annuals brighten flower beds
precisely. Suddenly it's June, and we expect the cosmos
to produce only perfection and the cycles of weather
to stand still for us. We expect all sunny days
and skies of deepest blue.
No rain or storms, no hail, nor gale,
no poison ivy, pestilence, nor itchy insect bites.
No black spot, mildew,
cold nor heat, no virus
and no hated flu.

Despite our dreams and fond desires, what will be,
will be. The universe won't stand still. The cycles
of Nature won't cease, and wisdom will teach us finally
to accept the rhythm of the cosmos, make no demands
and bring ourselves into harmony with it. Warmth,
sunshine and full bloom are only part of the pattern.

1993, SW Mo.

## *For Elliott*

You are the focal point of all my self,
more me than I am.
A crystal goblet, I.
You the good rich wine
that fills me sparkling to the brim.
Sun-drenched days,
ripening sweets, heady, fragrant,
mellowing then and aging.
All are you
and you in me.
When you are gone
I am the shattered wine glass
lying on the hearth.

1994, SW Mo.

# Back to the Sea Again

They say our ancestors of long ago lived by the sea,
swam in it, fished and boated, breathed the salt air.
They ate sea food, developed bigger brains and
better nervous systems. They became human beings.

Now you and I return once again to the coast.
We're drawn to it, as humans are, remembering
our ancient home. We are determined to dig our toes
in the sand. We dare to dip them in and out of
the cold advancing waves. They curl in white froth
up the beach, making a changing serpentine
pattern of long graceful curves. In warmer seas,
we swim, float and snorkel.

We always go in the fall. Like bears getting ready to
hibernate, we stuff ourselves with berries, fish, oysters,
crab, shrimp, mussels and clams. When in Maine or
Nova Scotia, we eat lobster rolls, crab rolls
and whole lobsters with lemon butter.

We exult in filling our chests again and again
with the fresh pungent air, exactly as our ancestors
must have done. We migrate often to the sea shore
like homing birds. We are almost as regular
in our seasonal migrations as salmon,
whales, sea lions, butterflies and birds.

August 28, 2002, Neskowin, Oreg.

# *Today*

Breathe in the fragrance of life today,
For its fragrance is all its own,
like no other.  Find its distinction.
Find its unity with other days.

The fragrance is there for the taking always,
the smell of the roses fresh before they wither.
Breathe in.  It's life.  It's for you.
Don't miss the fragrance of today.

1999, "Living Water", SW Mo.

# The World We Live In

The world we live in is partly our own creation.
The things we find wrong in the world
are caused by the same sins, the same weaknesses
and ignorance that we find in ourselves.

There is the world of our physical surroundings,
a room, an apartment, a house and lawn,
a block, a farm, a school, a church, a town.
We can make them places of beauty and order.

There is the world of our influence,
our family, our friends, our loved ones,
our acquaintances, our work place,
the groups where we belong.
We share in creating this world.

There is the world of our thoughts,
our attitudes, our emotions,
our words and our acts.
We can make that world
as fine as we can imagine.

*Power*, April-June, 1971, Christian Youth Publications

# *La Luz*
## *For Hank and Nancy*

The sun rises behind the Sandia Mountains as I watch
from west of the Rio Grande, from the place called
*La Luz*. The air is still and cold. I hear only the call and
twittering of birds, the distant roar of traffic.
The night lights of Albuquerque sparkle in the valley,
within the deep shadow of the peaks.

Overhead and east is a cover of broken clouds, lit red
from below by the rising sun.  To the southeast,
the sky is a clear and fragile eggshell blue.  Just above the
profile of dark mountains, the light shoots up through
horizontal streaks of clouds, changing every few seconds,
becoming brighter, less rosy, more white.

I do a few Yoga stretches, a few Tai Chi moves.
Breathing out, I bend toward the ground,
hands hanging loose, then raise them high above
my head as I breathe in.  Six times I do it, and I realize
an observer might think I was worshiping the sun.

This blessed place, *La Luz*.  Built and planned for the
unobstructed view of peaks, city lights, the sunrise.
It faces the east as Navajo hogans do, as many sacred
buildings do.  *La Luz* is Spanish for The Light.
I greet the sun with gratitude to the Creator,
thankful for another day of life,

thankful to be here, as others
before me have been for eons and eons,
time upon time, to watch the sun
come up again in this place.

January 28, 2002, Albuquerque, N.M.

## What I Am

Opening myself to the Creator,
eyes to see, ears to hear,
a mind to think,
hands to work, to write, to help,
a heart to beat, a heart to love,
a consciousness in a field of energy.*

*For the last line, thanks to Deepak Chopra.

*Thoughts and Inspirations*, March, 1978, First United Methodist
Church, Carthage, Mo.

## *On Every Beach*

Waves break
into white foam–
white fingers
reaching out rapidly
and crawling up
the hard-packed sand,
advancing,
then sinking in the sand
and receding back to sea
to meet the next
breaking white.
Pattern on pattern
of furling white foam,
ceaselessly,
eternally,
always new.

June 15, 1974, Hilton Head Island, S.C.

# This Morning Apart From Others

Overcast sun beats down through soft morning fog
in the creek valley.  Textured tree trunks stand tall.
One by one, leaves drift down slowly in the quiet air.
Red leaves glow on a lone maple, a large one.
On other trees, some leaves near ground are still green,
and farther away, a few maple leaves are golden.

Squirrels are busy loading their nests up high
with nuts--acorns, hickory, black walnuts.
They frisk their big bushy tails as they scamper
up the trunks and branches.

Later will be bright, sunny and warm,
but the fog, light and radiant red leaves
remaining on one tree make this
a jewel-like moment

November 5, 2001, "Living Water" SW Mo.

13

## *Starting Out*

Making a beginning is one of the best times of life.
When you begin with little or nothing, it is exciting
and scary. In spite of that knot in your stomach
of wondering how you will do, making a new start
is still one of the best times in life. You are leaving
the security of the things you can do, ready to see
what you can make of a whole new thing.
There is the challenge of it, the fear of not succeeding,
the hope of everything going great.
There are decisions to make, usually a great deal
of fruitless worry, thinking, planning, study,
work, work and more work.

We place high value on the "self-made" individual,
yet most who have been able to meet this challenge
so well did not make it entirely on their own.
Many of them insist they succeeded only
by relying on God for the strength and wit
and perseverance they needed for each day.

*Prayer:* Teach me to trust so completely in you, God,
that even while I am enjoying the great challenges
of life, I will realize how deeply I need your help,
minute by minute, hour by hour, day by day.

1980, SW Mo.

## *Grandfather of the Oregon Coast*

Haystack Rock at Cannon Beach is the grandfather,
massive and imposing, rising well over
two hundred feet above the sand and surf,
and around him in the breaking Pacific is
a whole family of miniature mountains, *his* family.
The grandmother, small, slender and serene,
the eldest son, a bit distant, with his own slender wife,
and up and down the coast, clusters of other sons
and daughters, nieces and nephews, with their own
offspring peaks. Northwest is the daughter with the
lighthouse. She's solid and built low to the sea.

Hovering around grandfather's knees are his sister and
the daughter who always wanted to stay close.

To be exact, he soars two hundred and thirty five feet
above the shoreline.  He is home and nesting place
to generation after generation of sea birds
and other creatures, including harlequin ducks,
black oyster catchers, pelicans, tufted puffins and
several kinds of cormorants and gulls.
In the tidal pools around Grandfather's feet,
hermit crabs scuttle.  Clinging to the rough black
lava rocks are ochre sea stars and sea anemones
of vivid green.  They open like flowers and
when touched, close immediately.

Grandfather has dominated the Oregon coast
for nobody knows how many moons.

There is none other like him.

August 23, 2002, Cannon Beach, Oreg.

16

# Nineteen Fifties, U.S.A.

The Twenties called their generation lost,
and lost they were in a changing world.
Lost was the veneration of old ideals,
lost too, the ways which once had guided men.
We of the Fifties are no longer lost.
We've found a way of living. It is not beautiful.
It has no grace, as the old ways once had.
We recommend it only on one virtue. It is
the only way. Not without sadness do we choose
the mode of practicality, but we see no other course.

Our guide is truth, our attitude clear-eyed.
We stoop not to despair. Dauntlessly, we face
the horrors that humanity has wrought,
daring not to hope for change. Yet with steadfast
patience, doing all *we* can, we must build a firm
morality within ourselves. That is the first step,
the one that *we* must take. For other generations--
well, the world lies steeping in its inhumanity.
But we of the Fifties must form our own integrity.
First, with a clarity of vision.
Second, without turning from the truth.
Third, by fulfilling obligations.
Fourth, with boundless mercy for all men.
And fifth, with strength to roust out evil from its nest.
That is the challenge fate has flung us.
We will not lay down the gauntlet in despair,

nor will we destroy ourselves in disillusion,
as did the children of the Nineteen Twenties.

Take up the challenge we must and will.
That is the heritage of our generation,
the generation of the Fifties, U.S.A.

April, 1952, during the Korean War, SW Mo.

(After I wrote *Nineteen Fifties, U.S.A.*, my husband was called to
active duty in the U.S. Army. He served in Korea from 1953 to 1954
in the U.S. Army Anti-Aircraft Artillery in support of infantry during
the hostilities and received a Field Commission as First Lieutenant
and Battery Commander.)

## Twenty-First Century, U.S.A.
## A Coda to Nineteen Fifties, U.S.A.

Now in November, 2001, with the Constitution and
declarations of our founding fathers to guide us, our
attitudes, patience and integrity in these United States
must be the same. Through all five steps the same, from
clarity of vision, without turning from the truth,
by fulfilling obligations, with boundless mercy for the
innocent and strength to rout out evil from its nest.
That is the challenge fate has flung to us. We will not lay
down the gauntlet in despair, nor will we destroy
ourselves with disillusion.

September 11 brought the unthinkable, inhuman
terrorist attacks on the Pentagon and World Trade
Towers in Manhattan , using loaded passenger jets as
explosive missiles. Nearly three thousand innocents from
eighty-six nations were murdered that day. Anthrax in
the mail to U.S. Senators and media personnel came next.
Our friends are gathering with us. The UN Assembly
meets in session now. We are fighting back and many in
the world join with us.

Take up the challenge we must and will. That is our
heritage in this Twenty-First Century. Pray God we and
all nations find the right direction, the way that leads to
order, justice, prosperity, freedom and to peace.

November 12, 2001, during the War on Terrorism, SW Mo.

19

## Secrets of the Deep

Islands in the lake--brilliant mounds of
autumn-colored leaves, vivid in the sunlight,
standing distinct in blue-gray water.

Islands in the lake--so much like people,
looking separate, looking distinct,
but connected underneath the surface.

In the depths underneath, we find
ourselves part of one whole.

1975, Holiday Island, Beaver Lake, Ark.

## *A Picture of Home*
(upon looking at an Andy Thomas oil painting)

Andy Thomas paints dappled sunlight
in bold white blobs,
remembering how the front porch looked,
the open door awash with the smell
of fresh-baked cinnamon rolls,
as his bike skidded to a halt
in front of the house on Garrison,
his boyhood home in Carthage,
his older brother Matt
dribbling a basketball,
white teeth and black hair glistening.

Andy does not paint the smooth skin
of his mother Olive Thomas,
but it is there in his memory,
behind the screen door,
and she is there, welcoming him.

Andy Thomas, the artist,
paints his memories for us.


November 9, 1991, Extemporaneous Poetry Writing Contest,
Second Place, Ozark Writers and Artists Guild, "A Poetry Affair"

## *Morning on Forest Beach*

The rain had stopped and I was walking northeast
up the beach. The tide was out, leaving a vast expanse
of hard-packed beach sloping very, very gently to the sea.
Water and sand were gray, with nothing to divide them
but the froth of white where the waves were breaking on
the shore. The storm had moved eastward out to sea,
making the eastern sky a deep and marvelous gray-blue.

Where the beach was wet, sometimes in tiny streamlets,
sometimes in vast, flat slopes, sometimes in pools and
shallow lakes left by the tide, the deep gray-blue of
the eastern sky repeated its color,
rich and deep against the flat gray of sand and sea.

I walked into this wet, reflected color, shiny, vast and
luminous. Was I walking into a new dimension,
another plane of life?

Fat sea gulls stood still upon the shiny, gray-blue sand,
enjoying the moment as much as I. Flocks of cheeping
sand pipers were running as if by automation,
their legs a blur of speed.

There was a fresh breeze blowing at my back. The sun
was warm upon my shoulders. In the dunes at my left,
golden sea oats were nodding in the wind.
I turned southwest to see bright blue sky showing

22

above the dark line of pines and palmettos.
The clouds were moving fast above my head.
All creation was frolicking in delight and wonder
at the morning. At sea, shrimp boats were casting
their nets close in to the shore. A red and white sail
billowed merrily, and children were riding their bikes
on the beach in great swooping arcs of freedom.

Yet all the creatures on the beach looked tiny
in that terrific landscape, and each figure
stood out distinctly, separate and alone
in the immensity of space and light.

August 13, 1970, Hilton Head Island, S.C.
*The Islander,* December, 1970, Hilton Head Island, S.C.

## Four A.M.

When you came to me in the middle of the night,
it was the last thing I wanted then.
I turned away, wanting nothing more
than to sink back down into sleep.
But my mind switched on a playback
of a stupid spat we'd had the night before.
Fiery coals of outrage and resentment
still glowed red beneath the ashes of remembrance.
I was not at all in the mood. I wanted no touching.
You touched me anyway. I lay rigid, thinking of
hated words you'd said, wishing you'd say
you were sorry, wishing you'd say you loved me,
wishing you would just say <u>something</u>.

You didn't speak. Another memory rankled, too.
I'd mentioned making love night before last.
Why didn't you come to me then?
Now I felt completely different.
So get me in the mood if you can, I thought.
Before long, you did. Bit by bit.
Soon I was helping and finally
it was good. It was very good.
That's the way love is.

## Whirring

Elusive hummingbirds sip
sometimes from our feeder–
and sometimes not.

## Revolt

The blooms are rioting
in my garden,
despite my orderly plans.

## July, 1992

The molehills are mountains
this summer.  Fine loose soil
mounded high in peaks.


Summer, 1992, SW Mo.

# Elegy for Kay

You loved white things. I'll always remember that.
White blossoms in your flower beds,
Snowy Cape Cod curtains billowing in a fresh breeze,
board-and-batten walls painted white for hanging art,
white cotton dresses banded with lace,
worn on summer afternoons and evenings,
dainty white satin bows tied to the graceful curves
of a brass chandelier, crisp blue-white linen
dancing with rainbows cast by heavy Waterford
crystal tumblers, a bunch of white silk
Lilies-of-the-Valley tied with a bow and laid
on a polished mahogany side table just so,
as if newly picked in the garden.

Freely you gave yourself to projects of the light,
but never did you have a baby of your own to love
and hold, a babe to soften you and make you laugh,
to humble you and teach you how to bend.
You were far too fragile and too brittle
for your clan or his.

We were far from ready for your death at fifty-five.
It happened after lunch. You refused to see the doctor
'til you'd bathed. You never had the chance.
Your heart stopped. Truly, you didn't have the heart
to go on. Stunned, your friends sent sprays

and pots and baskets of white flowers to our church,
the church you loved and served.

I'll miss your style, your special feminine elfin touch.
I'll miss your love of white things.
I'll miss you, Kay.

1990, SW Mo.

# Historic Homes Tour

No, I didn't see any ghosts or hear any ghosts, exactly, but here's how it was, Kay.

Carthage Historic Preservation was having a homes tour. Richard's house (your old house) was to be on the tour. He asked me to help. "Of course," I said. It seemed little enough to do at the time. He wanted me posted in your bedroom. He was thinking of selling the house.

I remember how you loved the place when your friends and next-door neighbors lived there, when you spent so much time together. We all enjoyed going there for parties. Richard bought the house as soon as it came on the market. You took so much pleasure in decorating, changing things around a bit, even buying some beautiful new furniture. Once you had the house fixed up, you had a lovely potluck dinner for eight or ten and showed us around the house. That's when I saw and admired the big upstairs bedroom with a fireplace and windows on three sides, the bedroom you had taken such pride in decorating. It was so individual, so typically you.

The house is a gracious place with a huge lawn, a long drive and a covered veranda supported by big columns of our local light gray stone. It faces not the road, but the old Southwest Missouri Railroad line between Carthage, Webb City, Joplin, Lakeside and Georgia City.

## Richard and Kay's House

First known as the McNerny House, built about 1912-1913,

now the home of Bill and Libby Wilson.

What caught our imagination most of all was the long
six-stall garage with black carriage lanterns Richard had
designed and built. It housed vehicles, boats, grills, tools,
lawn mowers, and all his camping, fishing and sports
equipment. We were right envious of that. We spent
so many good times in that house and in your previous
home next door. New Year's Eve, lovely dinners,
summer pot lucks, parties when you gathered
all your friends together and served them
yummy hors d'oeuvres, stylishly presented.

For the tour, I dressed suitably in period costume
as requested. I had to stand guard over your bedroom,
while the multitudes filed through, curious.
I had to keep your things from their depredations and
tendencies toward theft, point out the wooden shoe
your brother brought back from World War II,
stare at the row of animals on the mantel,
the whimsical bears with spectacles on their noses,
who looked so much like you,
stare as well at the heaps of pristine white pillows
of all shapes and sizes, eyelet, cutwork or edged with
lace. They were piled on the dainty white coverlet of
your bed and upon the Virginia Day Bed I had always
liked so well. It served as a couch in the living room of
your previous home. I had sat upon it or curled up
in one corner of it many times.

I had to point out the antique linens, point out Richard's
watercolors on the wall, the Japanese wood block print
above the pie safe, the delicate Swedish prints over the
dresser.  I even had to count eleven sterling silver objects
on its surface to make sure none were stolen,
the silver-backed brush and comb, hand mirror, pin tray,
a bunny, small covered boxes, et cetera.

As the day wore on, and I had to repeat the same story
over and over again in answer to the same questions, and
somehow counter the idle curiosity of the visitors,
my energy level and enthusiasm sank lower and lower.

It was too intimate in your bedroom.  I did not know
that being there among your things would be so hard,
would tire me so.  Kay, you were too much there.

June, 2002, SW Mo.

# *Growing*

We are fed as the trees are fed.
As great oaks stretch their roots,
burrowing deep in the earth,
absorbing water up though their roots,
taking mineral salts in solution,
so are we fed from the ground of our being,
from God our Father almighty,
sustainer of all of our life.

By an effort down through
the depths of ourselves,
down through conscious and unconscious levels,
grow the first feelers of inquiry
into the Source of our life.
Stronger they grow by the sustenance they find,
turning to healthy tendrils,
stretching and searching
into the mind and will of the Father,
until they become stabilizing, sturdy roots,
reaching for and drawing in
the never-failing nourishment of God
and grounded securely within him.

*Islander,* May, 1974, Hilton Head Island, S.C.

# *January Haiku #1*

I rise and join him
watching Mallards on the river.
Six drakes, six hens.

Winter, 2000, SW Mo.

# *Winter Morning*

Snow clings to the trunks
and caps each branch and twig,
the deck railings, too. Three inches high.
Snow covers the bluff to the dark river
where a dozen Mallards float. Six drakes,
six hens. Cardinals police the feeder here above,
watching the flutter of smaller birds.

Winter, 2000, SW Mo.

## *January Haiku #2*

Winter, and I rise
to join him watching Mallards
on the river.  We see a dozen.


Winter 2000, SW Mo.


## *A Little Conundrum*

For this occasion
I turn myself inside out
to reach you.
Why?
This I don't know.
I'm as mystified
as you by the need
I have to share myself.


1993, SW Mo.

34

# Canyon de Chelly
## (de Chelly is pronounced day shay')

Six hundred feet drops the red canyon wall
to the running water, slicks and wet sand
of Chinle Wash, reflecting the deep blue of the sky
and the light in its own lovely way,
watering the fresh green of cottonwoods and willows,
the peach and apple trees, chili peppers,
squash and beans, watering the sheep, dogs,
and horses of the Navajo
on the floor of enchanted Canyon de Chelly.
Wind, sand and water cut the canyon.
Wind, sand and water are all here today.

September, 1980, Canyon de Chelly National Monument, Ariz.

# Morning, Skyline Ridge

The trees stand silently today in their places.
They do not toss or turn. They stand as witnesses.
The spruce and cedar with their graceful swoops,
the straight trunks tall and elegant,
sunlight brightening the trunks this morning
against the dense gloom behind them.
A play of light and shadow, dark and bright,
with no sudden movement 'til now, when I observe
the agitated trembling of aspen leaves
above the metal roof of aqua green, like copper
exposed to air. A jet roars high overhead, unseen.
The aspens become still. Did the jet itself cause
the movement of the aspens as it passed?
Was the air disturbed? The Golden Rain tree
is vivid chartreuse arching in fresh furls above the roof.

Now I see a bit of movement, a waving of the
evergreens. I hear the drone of another plane
flying above. The one in sight heading north and
another to my right. Above the chimney float
a few fluffy clouds, forerunners. The leaves and
swooping branches are still again. It does seem
the planes have something to do with the movement.
A horsefly buzzes behind me. I hear a car
on Skyline Boulevard. My son comes out
of the woods shirtless, in dark blue shorts,
his chest and shoulders tan.
He's been meditating, doing Yoga.

He carries his gray blanket, my father's old
wool Navy blanket, tattered at the edges, with holes.

The trees stand silent once more.
Only the faintest movement with the faintest breeze.

1999, above the Columbia River, NW of Portland, Oreg.

## Two Kinds of People

"There are two kinds of people.
People who make problems and
people who solve problems."
I don't know who said it first, but I admire that
person's wisdom and keen observation of humankind.

Look about you. Some people create problems
wherever they go, getting hurt, getting angry,
crossing people off their lists, having feuds, quarrels
and fights, attacking and killing each other,
complaining, moaning, making everything difficult,
bearing a cloud of gloom, strife and chaos,
almost as if they enjoyed antagonism for its own sake.

Those who solve problems are often very quiet.
Sometimes you hardly notice them. They're busy
reading, learning, thinking, experimenting,
always working, always trying, figuring out answers,
watching and listening to people, enjoying the goodness
of life in the present moment, bringing people together,
making peace.

Where do you fit in most of the time?
Do you usually make problems or solve them?

*Power*, July-September, 1970, Christian Youth Publications

## The Source of All

My God, fountain of my spirit,
pouring your life through me
in a constant surge of majesty,
you are the source of living waters,
well-spring deep and never-ending,
goodness, joy and wisdom blending.
You are the fountain of my spirit,
pouring out your majesty,
the living waters of my life.

*Power,* April-June 1971, Christian Youth Publications,
St. Louis, Mo.

## Enchanted Islands

Mystic is an island in the mind of man,
a mythic, magic symbol of escape,
Stevenson's desert isle,*
*Swiss Family Robinson*'s delights,*
a dream of paradise.

An isle is separated from the main,
only joined by ferry, bridge or plane.
An island is separation in man's mind.
We crave separation from everyday routine,
from dealing with problems, people,
those we hate, even those we love,
from difficulties, temptations, evil,
most of all from facing the real self
and grappling with the *alter ego.*

Sometimes one must escape,
if only for a time, a time to think,
to dream, to ponder,
to rest, to play, to love,
perhaps to finally face
the inner man or woman
in the wind and constant surf
and loneliness of an island
and a beach.

1995, San Juan Islands, Wash. State
*Treasure Island*, Robert Louis Stevenson, *Swiss Family Robinson*, Johann Rudolf Wyse

40

# Sunday, Labor Day Weekend

Clear light here in front of Tolovana Inn,
colors dark and whites sharp against
smooth damp sand.  Receding surf and
wet reflected sky.  Movement everywhere.
A cyclist, determined walkers,
frolicking dogs, those chasing balls
and those briskly pacing their masters.
But on either side, at looming Haystack Rock
and south where less massive rocks thrust up
in the receding surf, I see patchy morning fog.
Here I stand in the light, glad to be alive
with the others.

September 1, 2000, Tolovana Park, Cannon Beach, Oreg.

## *An Honest Day's Work*

What kind of work is worth doing?
Healing and comforting, that's clear.
Teaching, if you are teaching what is true and
helpful. Serving others. Growing, making or
selling good, useful things. Creating beauty.
Conveying truth. Helping others to know themselves
and use their talents. Making the world a better place,
even in small ways. Loving and caring for others.
Building that which is good. Making cleanliness,
order and harmony from dirt and chaos.
Creating jobs, work and livelihoods by making
the wheels of industry go 'round, in an honest way,
without double-dealing or fraud, insuring always that
the end product is something good and useful.

Conserving and protecting the beauty and
balanced functioning of the natural world.
Bringing pleasure, joy and laughter
with a final effect of good upon the person.
Promoting health of body, mind and spirit.
Increasing man's knowledge and understanding.
Carrying the news that God loves each one.

Serving the people faithfully as part of a
just government.  Making peace.  Solving problems.
Doing any of these to the best of your ability,
working hard and giving full value for your wage,
you have justified your place upon the earth.

1982, SW Mo.


## Elizabeth Davis

Elizabeth Davis is a gem,
sparkling, original and rare.
Full of verve, she makes us dare
to edge out on that furthest limb.

*The simple verse above was written as an exercise at a 1989
meeting of the Carthage Writers Guild.  My friend Elizabeth Davis gave an
outstanding  program that day and asked everyone to write a four-line
poem during five minutes of silence.  Delightful Elizabeth Davis was a
constantly published poet, retired school teacher and librarian, a widow,
mother and grandmother.  She had wit, humor, humility and so much
charm.  I greatly miss the pleasure of her company as a fellow writer.*

1989, SW Mo.

# Portland, Oregon

### 1.

My granddaughter swims.
I dry off. She rests
on the edge of the pool.

### 2.

Small girl jumps in. Two years old.
Out again, she twists and turns,
black hair like cap.

# September, Oregon Coast

As sun sinks at Haystack Rock, peach fan with
violet base opens southwest in blue silk sky.
Below it, surf breaks white beyond a shimmering
swath of watered apricot satin beach.

September 2, 2000, Cannon Beach, Oreg.

# The Power and the Freedom

You gave us the power to create,
to create worlds of beauty, harmony and love
or ugly worlds of evil, hate and killing.
You have given us freedom to create
what we will.

The power to create comes directly from you.
It is divine. It is part of yourself.
It is a blessing and a gift.
It is a mystery we do not understand,
a challenge only a few ever meet.

How you trusted us to give us this power
and this freedom! Most of us have only moments
now and then of using it well.
Some never do.

1974, SW Mo.

# *Maui, Hawai'i*

How can one wax poetic
in the face of such perfection
as Kā'anapali Beach,
September 20, 2001?

We've made it to Hawai'i
for the first time to celebrate finally
our Fiftieth Wedding Anniversary
on the fourth of February, a trip
postponed because of two accidents.

We've made it from Oregon, where
we were packed to leave September 11th
when the world changed forever,
made it from San Francisco Bay,
where we managed to see old friends.

Lifelong fantasies are rewarded now
by the sight below our balcony
of palm fronds waving in the warm
tropic breeze, clear blue water, green grass,
colorful blossoms cascading everywhere.

The beach itself is a shock, though,
a narrow strip of steeply dropping
golden sand, a mere fringe of a beach
compared to the immensity and scale

of Cannon Beach on the Oregon coast
where we stayed just a week ago.

Soon we are swimming, turning and splashing
like porpoises in the delightful refreshing water.
(Oregon's always frigid.)  My toes stick up and out as
I float happily on my back, buoyant in the salty water.

## *Tunnel Vision*

I fly through the tunnel of light
toward a brighter glowing light.
Kindly, oh yes, kindly light.

Energy cuts through excuses like a laser.
All is revealed. Merciless, blue white,
fluorescent light, revealing all flaws in me,
the reasons why. Motives all revealed
for what I did. No place to hide.
No place, no place.

Everything clear in the light,
Beneficent light, bright with energy.
All knowing, all known.
Brilliant light.
Golden with wisdom, all wisdom.
God is light.

Now I see face to face,
myself and Creator, the Light,
glowing, and brighter than the sun.

1987, SW Mo.

48

# Some Early Poems

## Harvest Ball

At the pumpkins' party on Halloween
they all rolled in and saluted the queen.
They danced the Shag and the Highland Fling
'til the cornfield clock said, "Ting-a-ling-ling".

*A dance called "The Shag" was all the rage in 1938, the year my parents and I moved from Kansas City, Missouri, to Forest Hills, Queens, Long Island, New York, and I entered the third grade at the School in the Gardens, P.S. 101. I loved my lively and inspiring red-haired teacher, Miss Ackerman. She asked each student to write a Halloween verse. When mine was published in the January 31, 1939 World's Fair Issue of the school's TOWER Magazine, I got so firmly hooked on writing I've never recovered.*

*When I left in May, never to return to Forest Hills again, sweet Miss Ackerman wrote on my report card (which I found just the other day), "We are losing our very best pupil." She definitely gave my life a direction.*

## The Sound of Singing

The voices lift high and then low
like a rippling waterfall,
low like an organ in the twilight glow.
Then higher they grow and die, then live again.

*I heard singing and music often as I grew up, for my mother was a singer actively involved in study, practicing and performing. I recently found this childhood effort dated September 2, 1939.*

49

## Pink Dogwood

Fingers of a miraculous rose-red hue,
unearthly in their beauty, are reaching for
a drop of the azure blue of the heavens
to fill their pink cups.
'Til my soul be as lovely as these,
then I, too, will reach toward the skies.

May I be as wise as these blossoms divine
reaching up, ever upward to glory unknown.
Blossoms of God,
let your story be mine.

*La Fuente*, 1948, Long Beach, Calif.

*It was April, 1942, my first spring in Southwest Missouri since
I was six years old. We were living in Joplin that year, and I was in the
eighth grade at North Junior High, a happy year for me. Daddy was
working as a construction electrician at Camp Crowder a few miles south.
Mother sang there often, doing concerts, starring in a production of
"Toyland" at Christmas, and also at the USO.*

*I was walking alone on the lawn of my aunt and uncle's home
at Mission Hills Farm, now the campus of Missouri Southern State
University, when I saw the small flowering tree in full bloom, petals
silhouetted against a deep blue sky. I stood thunderstruck and inspired,
ran indoors for pencil and paper, then scribbled down a rough first draft.
"Pink Dogwood" was the first poem I wrote because I couldn't help it,
because I was overcome and simply had to pour out my feelings and
reactions to the stunning sight before my eyes.*

## *Indian Summer*

I could live forever in a wonderful world
made up of a clear blue sky
and a haze hanging over the Palisades,
so dark and foreboding and high.

A summer haze on an autumn day,
whose air is as warm as June.
Indian Summer in old New York,
made to keep hearts in tune.

November 11, 1943, Manhattan, N.Y.


## *Waiting*

To him who waits
all things must come,
according to my mother,
but laughing hours of life are past,
and hours of sadness, hours of tears,
have filled a space too vast.

*La Fuente*, 1948, Long Beach, Calif.
*Islander*, April, 1972, Hilton Head Island, S.C.

# A Walk on the Beach

In a lonely world and weary,
my sad heart alone is weeping,
but the sea mists all around me
give no token of the sound.
Could they but know my sorrow
at the wide world's cruel blunders,
then they with me would sorrow
at the world's eternal wrongs.
But the cold gray mists are heedless;
they are blind to all my grieving,
and I find my solace only
in their calm neutrality.

1940's, Calif.
*Islander,* November, 1973, Hilton Head Island, S.C.

# *Pearls*

I tossed my pearls into the sky,
my shining pearls, so bright, so white,
and tied with a scarlet ribbon.
I caught them as they laughed down at me,
with eager fingers, my fingers laughing, too.

I caught my pearls and said to my heart
(the part of my heart that remembers),
"How like the pearls that come down to us
from heaven above, so far above.

"We share these pearls, celestial gifts,
we give them to one another,
so that all may know of these different pearls
that come from another realm,
that shine so bright in the sun,
so white and bright in the sun."

*La Fuente*, 1948, Long Beach, Calif.

53

# Query

Which way, dear child, which way? The easy path?
The common road? Or will you scale the heights?
Your youth, like birth's first aftermath,
is through, and finished are your childhood rites.
Now weave the silken threads so lately spun
into a tapestry of life. Be quick.
Be deft, and show me when your work is done.
Oh dye your silk in dreary hues and pick
the taken track of sweet nonentity.
Have peace of mind, contentment, love and friends
or surge creating to celebrity,
through misery. Give all to art that rends
the heart and paints with blood. I care not which,
but in discernment live, in truth be rich.

*National Anthology of High School Poetry,* 1948
*La Fuente,* 1948, Long Beach, Calif.

# Lélia

Atop the craggy steeps of Nantua
is poised an opalescent-shaded stone,
reflecting passioned moods of Lélia,
the fallen angel, pensive and alone,
imprisoned deep in unrelenting stone.
Enchanted by its shifting lambent hues,
Nantua's fate her mystic power imbues.

Far 'neath the height within a shaded dell
a shepherd sleeps. Like sheep, his will is shorn
as drifts into his dream, like smoke, the spell
of Lélia. Desire for her is born.
Enticed, he leaves his loved maid forlorn
to hue the rock wherein the siren dwells.
His every stroke her lonely craving quells.

*La Fuente*, 1947, Long Beach, Calif.

## Tribute to Mrs. Minami

*At Woodrow Wilson Senior High in Long Beach, California,
it was my great good fortune to have a superb English Teacher named
Mrs. Minami. I believe her given name was Helen. She was a
demanding, exciting, unforgettable teacher with the highest of
standards. She led us deep into classic literature and asked us to
write poetry in several specific forms. I did my best to comply. The
above narrative poem called "Lélia", "At the Piano","Your Eyes" and
the sonnet on the previous page called "Query" are all the results of
her assignments. Mrs. Minami, I close my eyes and see your lively
intelligent face, your black hair pulled smoothly back from your*

*forehead in an elegant French twist and your dark eyes sparkling behind your thick glasses as you question us, explain to us and pace up and down the rows between our desks.*

*I blush as I remember how you carefully did your best to handle my innocent but insistent questions about the meaning of Hamlet's remarks to Ophelia, despite grins and titters from other more sexually informed students.*

*Your passionate, caring, well-educated mind and sudden humor, your love of life, literature and everything fine, your warm but far from sentimental heart, obvious culture and great enthusiasm were all encased in a neat, stylish ladylike person perfectly dressed for the classroom in quiet clothes of excellent quality.*

*You made your mark on me. Thanks for asking us to do our best and giving us yours. Thank you, Mrs. Minami.*

## At the Piano

From 'neath my trembling hands such sound does rise
that I pour out the passions of my soul
into another's dream.  Then dies
within my spell the last full roll,
and he who wrote and I who played are whole.
His music, spirit's blood, I drank and found
fulfillment in communion of eternal sound.

1947, Long Beach, Calif.

*My hands always shook dreadfully when I played the piano in public, especially when I was playing from memory.  Yet, music is extremely important to me, live performances in particular.  I have a grandson now who can do all that I wanted to do, but could not.*

56

# *Thoughts on an Evening Walk*

Night's blue shadows rose from the earth
to veil the sunset's flaming glory,
and my soul had soared to equal heights.
I gazed into the heavens, where the clouds,
like dreams of the Great Unknown
within Man's spirit, were a flocculent mass
whose wool burned quickly with a rosy fire,
the better to illumine in Man's sight
the splendor which his life might be.
Their faint and pearl-like glow,
in that one moment, was shot with flame,
and as they dimmed into space,
all desire was in them incarnate.

Now the moon shone down as pure and lovely
as the Spirit, serene and beautiful, glorious
and strong, which might make our beings as radiant
as its own, would we but rocognize its presence.

*Islander,* January, 1974, Hilton Head Island, S.C.

# *Flight*

I saw a sea gull flying high.
'Bove Long Beach streets I saw him fly.
His wings were white and tipped with black.
His flight was graceful, fluid, slack.
I saw him fly and knew the strain
of longing to be free again.

*La Fuente,* 1948, Long Beach, CA
*Islander,* April, 1972, Hilton Head Island, S.C.

# *Homecoming*

I come to my home in the evening
discouraged and weary with care.
My eyes turn towards the windows.
I see love and light shining there.

A wonderful feeling of peace
comes over my world-saddened heart,
for I know with a knowing of gladness
that loved ones will take my part.

Projects built only of dream stuff
I tell to those I love best.
On their word and honest opinion
my own decision will rest.

I work in my home to make comfort
for all those who share it with me.
I work for my family and love them.
I forgive them as they forgive me.

I drop every last rag of pretense
or striving for fortune or fame.
They know all my faults and my virtues.
Their love leaves no room for blame.

Should all of my friends turn against me,

should all of the world know my guilt,
here lies love past all understanding
on which home, a true home, is built.


*Here's the story of "Homecoming", the poem above. I was sinking toward a D in Home Economics, Sewing, at Woodrow Wilson Senior High School, in Long Beach, California, even though I was doing my best. Not until my emerald green wool dress was finished and I put it on to wear to a party, did I realize I'd put the side zipper on the wrong side. I wore it anyway. Sewing that zipper in and working with the bulky wool had been so hard, I couldn't face ripping it out and putting it back in on the other side.*

*On Monday, my Home Ec teacher gave us an assignment to write something about what home meant to us. "This is my chance to bring up that grade," I thought.*

*I decided to write a poem and pulled out all the stops I could think of to make up for my deficiencies as a seamstress and win my teacher's heart.*

*It worked. She loved this poem, gave it an A+ and read it aloud to the class. At the end of the semester, she gave me a B- in the course. Without this poem, I might not have learned, upon opening my graduation program, at the Long Beach Municipal Auditorium, that a friend and I were named co-Salutatorians in our graduating class of four hundred and six. For me, it was a complete surprise and a tremendous thrill.*

# Poi'pū Beach, Kaua'i, Hawai'i
## September 28, 2001

How can this paradise be true?
How can it be so gorgeous? Everything here.
The very stuff of dreams, the greatest fantasies,
the very texture, warp and woof of them.
The bluest, many-colored sea, navy, cobalt, turquoise,
shading to lightest aqua in the shallows. The whitest surf.
Satisfying crashes and roars, breaking many times
before reaching the beach. Black lava rocks. Golden
sand. Cooling breeze like a presence of its own. Tall
waving palms. Torches at night lighting up the grounds,
even the surf itself lit by lights and moon, full moon,
of course, shimmering in a pathway on the water,
seen from the dining room.

Even the architecture, this succession of simple
three-story stucco buildings following the shore,
with balconies looking out on beach and sea.
So well-planned. Non-obtrusive, designed for this site
after the 1992 hurricane, which blew down so many
things on Kaua'i, wrecking this hotel, uprooting trees,
scattering chickens all over the island, so that now
there are roosters, hens and chicks everywhere. A
previous big hurricane struck ten years earlier. This
Paradise is vulnerable to so many kinds of destruction.
Earthquakes, erupting volcanoes, typhoons, *tsunamis* and
floods. Invaders bearing strange diseases, monster plants

and animals to overwhelm the native species.
And now this! Islamic terrorists hijack planes full of
passengers in Boston and New York, crash them like
missiles into the World Trade Center in Manhattan,
collapsing the twin towers, dive bomb the Pentagon and
kill nearly three thousand people from eighty nations,
creating a ripple effect around the globe, causing our
stock market to nose dive, even after the four-day shut
down, and reducing U.S. air travel by at least one-third.
Airlines lay off one hundred thousand, and these islands
of Hawai'i, twenty-five hundred miles from anywhere
else in all directions, their sugar cane industry already
destroyed by Third World competition, see their tourist
industry crumbling before their eyes. The citizens of
this Paradise fear for their jobs, their businesses,
their livelihood.

After a cascade of merry giggles, the charming young
desk clerk with a blossom in her hair tells us gravely,
"Nothing will ever be the same again." The beach, the
surf, the reefs and rocks, the breeze, the birds, sea life and
bright fish will still be here. The hula will be danced.
Palms will wave and plants will fruit and flower lavishly.
"Oh, we won't starve," a strong young bell man tells us
with a shrug, but there are worried furrows between his
brows. Will this hotel and others on Kaua'i still be open
entertaining guests in three years' time? Who knows?
It is Paradise today. The future is a question mark.

## *The Fire of Love*

Between two, there's a spark,
a burst of energy, a dancing electric arc.
That spark can grow to passion, ignite
into a raging flame consuming all before it.

Without the fuel and oxygen of tender love
and patience, faithfulness and kindness,
the flame sputters, gutters and dies out.

Neglect or cruelty, cutting words,
betrayal, horrid violence, turn it to ashes,
bitter, cold and dead.

Nourished every day, the flame becomes
a burning coal, a glowing ember,
lovely and warm, that lasts as long
as life itself, with first spark
and raging fire always to remember.

November 9, 1991, Betty Cooke Rottman's workshop,
Ozark Writers Guild, *A Poetry Affair,* SW Mo.

63

## The Gem Time of Christmas

The best of Christmas is Christmas Eve
when all is dark and still, except for
dancing candles and lights glowing on the tree.

The work is done at last.  We take a moment
to rest, to savor the fragrance of pine, juniper
and spice, to play and sing the old carols,
the merry and sacred music from the past,
from other lands, to read again the ancient stories
and ponder their meaning, drawing close in love,
cherishing the beauty of Christmas Eve,
the time of peace, enjoying the colorful gifts
wrapped and sparkling underneath the tree,
enjoying anticipation of tomorrow and
the time of being together in festivity.

1972, SW Mo.

## Simple Work

I was busy with projects and people,
frantic with business and bills
I had time for nothing but worry,
How could I snap the green beans?

Other matters awaiting
were far more important, I thought,
but at last I fled from heavy thinking
and headed for the yard.

Comfortably stretched on a lawn chaise,
under deep shade of a tree,
with a newspaper bearing the beans on my lap
I permitted my fingers to work.

A fresh green smell arose from the beans.
They satisfied me with their snaps.
The heap in my lap diminished,
and I found I began to relax.

A wren sang in the redbud.
A light breeze cooled my arms,
Green life, like that all around me,
broke sharply under my hands.

Affairs so worrisome faded.
I forgot what they were about.
I was happy, serene and contented
in the rest of my simple work

Summer, 1968, SW Mo.

*Thoughts and Inspirations,* March, 1978,
First United Methodist Church, Carthage, Mo.

## *Year's Difference*

A year ago, this boy's only self-assertion
was a fluttery rat-tat-tat somewhere below my waist.
Now, at eight month's old, he's busy with diversion,
leaving a wake of havoc in his eager haste
to do all, feel all, see all
and put all into his curious mouth to taste.

January, 1956, SW Mo.

# Mother's Name

Help is the name of my mother.

"How can I fix this?" "I'll fix it," she says.

"My garden's a mess." "Give me a hoe."

"What shall I do?" "Read this and pray."

"How can we go?" "We'll stay with the kids."

Whenever she comes, it's with her arms full.
Bouquets of flowers, a quart of green beans,
dresses she's made for Lisa and me,
an armload of mending that I couldn't do,
food from the garden, "Let's freeze it," she says,
jars full of jelly, flats of young plants.

Whenever we're sick, she brings us a cure.
Gladly she gives. We're glad to receive.
Help is the name of my mother.


1969, Mother's Day, SW Mo.

## *For Lisa,* Six Years Old

Your sweet and loving cuddly ways
brighten up our nights and days.

There's just a little stubborn streak
that makes us want to scream and shriek.
It's just a little streak we'd like to take out.
Do you know a remover that takes out a pout?

When the only thing a girl can see
is what she wants to do,
is there a kind of eyewash
that will make her vision true?

Do you think we could unplug her ears
so she could *hear* the reasons
why bathing suits cannot be worn
in cold and icy seasons?

Streak-remover, eyewash,
unplugger for the ears.
Tell us where to get them
and banish all our fears.

And after we have used them,
we'll all cuddle up with bliss
and give our darling little girl
a great big hug and kiss.

February, 1964, SW Mo.

## A Place to Play

I shan't forget my first eager dash
over scorching wooden slats of the
boardwalk path, through the dunes
and waving heads of sea oats
onto the dazzling wide-angle, far open
space of Forest Beach at low tide, sloping so
gently to the breaking edge of the sea that
the beach seemed nearly flat, incredibly wide,
the bowl of the sky incredibly vast above.

And then I saw it, the cause of my joy,
the theme of all other times we would
spend on this beach, the temper and mood
of this special place; a patch of red high in
the air, a quadrangle really--red, red with
a white dot, swooping and bobbing, a kite!
Below on the beach, a small figure running,
and between them, the barely discernable
connecting fine line of the string.

Far up and down the beach, other kites flew
and blithely sailed in the breeze, strained
at their strings, soared up and up, or suddenly
plunged on a downdraft.  Blue, yellow, orange,
each with its white dot in the center.

At once, our children begged for instant cash
to buy kites of their own and dashed away to
the shops nearby, soon to tear back to the beach
and gleefully set their own kites asail, delighted
as the string wound rapidly off their spools
and the kites strained up to high-flying clouds in the sky.

Year after year, kites flew high over Forest Beach,
especially when a brisk breeze sprang up from the sea
in the evening between sunset and dark.  We would all
go out on the beach and fly our kites in happy communion
with tiny figures far away connected
to bright quadrangles dancing high above.

In the daytime, we all sailed Frisbees in between swims,
food and *siestas*.  We played like children, especially my
work-worn husband, young again in his floppy white beach
hat, flipping Frisbees to the kids, running,
laughing and leaping to catch the returns
as eagerly and merrily as a carefree young pup.

Always after dark, there were fireworks on the beach,
which I enjoyed, and firecrackers, which I never liked
because they broke the natural sounds of the beach,

broke the roar and rustling income of the surf,
the sucking whisper as it receded,
the incomparable sound of the sea breaking on the shore, a
sound always precious and soothing to me.
Yes, soothing even when the sea was wild and rough
and high, for in the sound of the sea, I always lost myself.

Only there on that beach was the time always right
for fireworks and Frisbees and high-flying kites.
Never a closed season or a wrong age
for light-hearted fun on this special island,
where all four of us were children, coming and going
as we pleased, summer after summer.
Sometimes I wish the summers and the childhood
would never come to an end.

Summer, 1974, Hilton Head Island, S.C.

## *Two of My Angels*

Having known fear, Laurel wanted
to make me unafraid of this surgery.
Having walked through the valley,
she wanted to take the dark shadows from me.
She entrusted me with a precious commodity,
her own well-tested trust in our doctor,
confided her confidence in him,
encouraged me with her courage.

Laurel phoned the nurse named Mary,
and the two of them worked together then,
Laurel sending daily cards and telephoning love
from home, Mary the angel nurse of the night,
wrapping my cold feet in warm flannel
at four in the morning, inserting a quick expert shot
to kill the pain, placing a pillow just right in the small
of my back, followed by a ten-minute conversation on
books, authors and drama as the shot took its effect.

She reported daily to Laurel, but on her days off,
Mary phoned me, too, just to see how I was.
One day, she brought two of her own treasured books
for me to read and enjoy, the first a recent Christmas gift
about the sea, the second filled with poetry and drawings
by a friend, surmounting tragedy.  Mary shared
a deep part of herself with me, as Laurel did, too,
showing me how much they cared.

When I went home, the mail man brought
cheery cards and messages from Laurel--"Welcome home",
"Don't overdo", "I know you'll feel stronger
every day". She sent a box of note sheets
completely covered with flowers for thanking all
the others who showered me with love, and on Monday,
Laurel came herself, bearing a plate of cookies
and her own living example of how well I was going
to turn out. She was wrapping me up with
the follow-up visit, checking me out to make sure
I was okay in every way--attitudes, habits,
body and mind, ready to set me straight
if I hadn't been progressing right along
in successful convalescence.

Used by God because they cared about me,
because they wanted to be instruments of loving mercy,
(and spiced just right with wit and fun),
Laurel and Mary were two living angels to me
when I needed honest-to-God living angels the most.

About 1975, SW Mo.

73

## *Go Down Pride*
### Lyrics for a Gospel Hymn (Music Wanted)

We made a city, O Lord.
We made a city, O Lord.
We made a city, O Lord.
And we're trapped in the city we made.

We built clear up to the sky.
We built clear up to the sky.
We built clear up to the sky,
but we can't see the sky no more.

We had everything runnin' so smooth,
everything runnin' so fine,
everything runnin' so nice,
but it ain't runnin' nice no more.

I guess we built on the wrong foundation.
We didn't build on your Rock.
We built this city as our own creation,
and Lord, O Lord, we was proud!

We see very clear what we made.
We see that it ain't no good.
Set us free from our pride and our greed.
Show us the way to renew.

The world that you made is so good.
The Word that you sent is so right.

Show us the way to live in your world,
lovin' the earth and lovin' your people,
livin' in rhythm with your creation
to fit in with your great plan.


## *Diggledy Down*, *Lyrics for a Child's Singing Game (Needs a Catchy Tune)*

Diggledy down,
kur ploo, kur plow.
Who is the happiest in the town?
Diggledy diggledy,
higgledy piggledy.
Do not forget to look around.

Diggledy down
kur ploo, kur plown.
'Tis the season you have the reason
to smell the flowers, build tall towers,
run a quick mile, pull out a smile,
make a pie, look at the sky.

Diggledy diggledy,
higgledy piggledy.
Put out your hand, make life grand.
Diggledy up, kur ploo, kur plop,  kur plam!

*Both songs written 1978, SW Mo.

## Waiting to Make Camp

Dressed for cool-weather floating, I stand waiting
knee-deep in the stream, my feet in tennis shoes
planted firmly on the rocky bottom, jean legs wet,
but water a pleasant temperature, not too cold,
hands on my hips beneath the vinyl poncho
covering my life jacket and falling nearly
to the water, a gentle rain beating softly
on the tight hood and shoulders.

I've found our camping gear left on the gravel bar
near Jim's Bluff while we floated the first five miles
of the Buffalo River--fast and tricky, with big boulders,
white water, but too low for heavily-loaded canoes,
weather dry 'til just before Jim's Bluff.
Now, grateful for the poncho which gives me
such curious shape and comfort, I stand waiting
for my three companions, husband, daughter
and her boyfriend, to guide them to our gear.

I'm contented in the soft rain, suddenly aware
of everything about me in this moment,
everything coming at me through my five senses
with impact so startling I can't account for it.
I hear an occasional scrape of aluminum on rock
as they drag the canoes behind them up the river
through the rapids, around the bends we shouldn't
have floated. We should have stopped at the mouth

of the stream and turned up it to reach the
gravel bar where our camp gear was waiting.
Sometimes, I hear a call, or think I do, but
the rain beats softly, muffling other sounds,
and the poncho hood is tight around my ears.

Now I see them, three khaki-ponchoed figures
as oddly-shaped as I, seeming to float towards me
through the rain and into the mouth of the stream,
towing canoes behind them.  I see these bizarre
figures through white curls of fog rising in cool air
from the warmer water.  Against the dark trees
of a looming bluff, they move towards me
through the fog, like figures in a dream
or a Japanese wood block print, as I stand
peacefully waiting, absorbing the scene,
the gentle steady rain, the fast-coming dark.

May, 1976, Buffalo River, NW Ark, Lisa's graduation float.

## *In Our Fifties*

My sweet, I think we near the harvest time,
though we still toil and labor in the field
and wonder if our efforts have no rhyme,
logic or purpose to be finally sealed
with peace of goal attained or good work done.
Corn and grain are taken to the mill.
Fruits and vegetables full ripe in sun,
preserved and canned for all to eat their fill,
pumpkins bright and rows of jars to see.
Yet you and I in middle age work on
and cannot view the reaping that's to be.
Work on we must until our time is gone,
regardless of the ways of other men,
and hope we bring a goodly harvest in.

1986, SW Mo.


## *Harvest Still Life*

Ripe fruits glistening,
sweet rich moisture in each cell.
Work brought to an end


1987, Regional Poetry Retreat, Ginger Blue Resort, SW Mo.

# Autumn Day on Elk River

Quiet and slow flows the river,
golden leaves floating easily on its surface,
deep blue-green water mottled only
by the ripples of the breeze blowing gently.
Inexorably, the water goes.

Do not be deceived today by the slowness
of its flowing. It flows, moves,
the current never stopped,
only turned a bit, deflected.

Life is like this river.
We may turn its course somewhat,
ride jubilant on its currents for awhile.
We may fight the turbulent water,
but never can we stop its flow.

Change will come, <u>does</u> come
around each bend, but the river of life
flows on from birth to death
and far beyond.

We enjoy the river best when we learn at last
to steer gracefully with its flow.

1983, Ginger Blue Resort, McDonald Co., SW Mo.
*1984 Lenten Devotional, Entering the Emptiness,*
First United Methodist Church, Carthage, Mo.

## *House of Our Fortieth Year*

House, you stand there solid in the hillside
by the labor and skill of builder, workmen
and mechanics who knew how to make you solid.
But first you grew in the mind of my husband,
in his dreams and mine, grew from that first day
we climbed the slope together to the ancient oaks
and white-barked sycamores and looked down
on the creek going by, saw the Blue Heron fly.
House, you grew within us then, took form
in our minds, and he worked all one year
designing and planning and drawing,
worked with the builder, who drew plans of his own,
worked with me as we made plans together.
Your stone corners grow up from the earth.
You jut from the slope like the prow of a ship
commanding the waters. You are real, our house,
solid in your three dimensions at last.

February 12, 1991, our southern Missouri home "Living Water",
named in reverence for creative inspiration, the flowing river we see,
and Frank Lloyd Wright's architectural masterpiece "Falling Water",
a home jutting out above a waterfall.

# *A Burst of Blue*

Wild phlox spangle the hillside with violet blue
down to the damp deep of the dells. Halfway down,
four-petalled dogwood flowers open white,
floating above dark brown limbs. At the foot
of the bluff, the creek flows by, leaving
gravel bars behind. Too soon the blue of phlox
and white of dogwood will disappear. We, too,
will fade and wither long before we wish.
We'll disappear from this place. The wild phlox
will bloom again. So will the snowy dogwood.
Like them, we shall flower again
in the right time and season.

Spring, 1994, "Living Water", SW Mo.

81

## *First Light*

I walk softly on my deck at first light
as birds sing and call in the trees.
I walk softly, so as not to intrude.
It is still *their* world at this early hour,
the natural kingdom.
A half moon hangs high in the southwestern sky.
The sun rises in the east. Through the trees,
I barely see it. A Great Blue Heron flies up
from the brown waters of the flooded creek,
wings spread wide to gain height.
I'm seldom up at this hour.
It is still the world of creatures
and growing plants. Water flowing. Cool air.
The moon in the sky. The world of nature.
I must walk softly at this sacred hour.

1992, "Living Water", SW Mo.

# Sunday Morning on the Beach

Morning light reveals each object, each creature
on the beach in high relief. Blue sky overhead
with thin scattered clouds drifting. At sea level
patches of morning fog float through clear air.
Continuously the surf roars on this beach
and many places along the Oregon coast.
One does not hear each breaking wave distinct
from all others. The surf is high today,
higher than yesterday, the swells larger,
tumbling into frothy white.

Every creature has its own peculiar gait, a signature
unique as a fingerprint, the rhythm of the legs showing
clear against the background of smooth damp sand,
sandpiper legs almost a blur of motion, gull steps
much slower and more deliberate, unleashed dogs
frolicking and bounding in and out of the water
in gleeful delight as they chase balls and Frisbees.

White tennis shoes show up the brightest on humans.
A  runner lopes along in a yellow tank and blue shorts.
An older man in a white patterned shirt walks,
holding leashes of his two small dogs, one black,
the other white with a fluffy tail and large black spots.
Two little girls in bright pink wade out in
the frigid water.  A  dark-clad man in shorts and
leather sandals keeps a firm grip on the leads

of his brisk-pacing German Shepherds,
striding with their pull.  All three move quickly
down the beach with a white-shirted woman.

All is peaceful here this morning.  Against my face,
the air is cool and fresh.  The gulls squawk.
Life is living, moving, happy to be alive
this morning in this place.  And I am, too.

Labor Day weekend, 2001, Tolovana Beach, Tolovana Park,
Cannon Beach, Oreg.

# *How Was It, Anyway?*

"What would be hard for them to do?" thought God.
"What can I command them that will be
against their human natures? Yes, I shall command
them not to steal, kill, lie, commit adultery,
make graven images, bow down before false gods
or covet their neighbors' things. They'll struggle
throughout eternity with these commands.
They'll never make it."

Or was it this way? "I'll show them how to live
the best life," thought God. "I'll make a chart for them
that shows the way to the greatest good, the greatest joy.
Moses is my man. I'll give him the chart, and he
can pass it on to the others. Matter of fact,
I'll speak to everyone I can, everyone who
turns to me and listens.

"Just a few simple rules will keep people healthier and
happier, make life much more harmonious and pleasant
on earth. Following these rules will greatly reduce
turmoil, needless suffering and pain. It's all been caused
by stealing from each other and bearing false witness
with lies, worshiping false and evil gods, by envy, greed,
murder, rape, battering and torture, by harming
children and other innocents, by committing adultery
and wrecking lives and hearts down through
the third, fourth and fifth generations.

"If Moses and the others can't get through to them,
I'll go myself and say, 'Do for others what
you would have others do for you.  Love me
with all your heart and mind and soul.
Love your neighbor as yourself.'

I'll give them all the guides they need
for the good, the joyous and creative life."

*Power,* July, 1970, Christian Youth Publications

## *Sisters*
### *To Some of My Kindred Souls*

I never had a sister until I had you.
Now my sisters are thousands
and hundreds of thousands.

You believe in me, support me,
send me birthday cards in December,
never let me down.  You understand.

I'm not perfect. You're not perfect.
Who said we were?

But we're trying. We have goals,
common goals and personal secret goals.

I know you'll help me reach my goals
and I will help you, too.

We are sisters, and I love you.

1990, SW Mo.

# Wheel of the Universe
## A Prayer Wheel

*Try using this as a tool and starting point for meditation or prayer. It can be arranged in a circle, with God on top. Read clockwise or counter clockwise. Or, put God in the center, connecting everything with equal signs. Add other words, such as Creator, The Force, Father, Mother, Son, Christ, Holy Spirit. Your definitions. Your understanding. Your prayer.*

God
equals
Love
equals
Joy
equals
Life
equals
Growth
equals
Energy
equals
Power
equals
Light
equals
God

1995, SW Mo.

# *Canvas Surfer*

First, step into the water, dizzying underfoot
as the waves advance and recede on the sand.
Ankle deep, knee deep, walking out to sea,
white foam bubbling and boiling against me.
Now hip deep and feeling the tow made by
the wind on the water, pulling me parallel to the beach.
The air mattress drags heavy behind me and
I lift it clear of the water. Now the great struggle,
pushing ahead, fighting my way past the tow,
facing to sea, resting my arms on the
striped red and white canvas,
using it to float through breaking waves,
to shield my face through crashing surf.

Now quickly, up, up before the next breaker,
hoisting my body up on the canvas,
lying flat on my stomach, paddling fast out to sea,
both arms like oars, enduring the waves that
break over me, face down. Will I be wiped out
by the next tremendous wave or make it through
to easy water? Still paddling with all my strength,
there, turn quickly now and face the shore.
A moment's rest, feeling the swells beneath me.
Ahead, swimmers struggling through the breakers.
Am I too far out? Crane to the left. Crane to the right.
Where are the big ones breaking? Paddle in a bit.

I'm lifted by a swell. Will it take me?
No, it crashes just ahead.
Wait a bit more as the waves roll beneath me.

There, the water thunders down just behind my heels.
That's it! Grip the canvas, go. Shooting shoreward,
down and forward,
skimming smooth water, ahead of the wave,
almost like flight,
so fast, so light,
powered with a dynamo under my knees
and under my thighs,
a thrust I can't see,
shooting me past startled swimmers
who gape as I go hurtling by.

The beach appears suddenly right before
my startled eyes, my face skimming level toward
the fast-approaching sand.
Now I feel its friction beneath me,
catching and turning me.

I drag to a reluctant halt, exhilarated.
I'm beached. I'm beached,
no longer sea-borne, but beached,
once more a creature of land.

1968, Hilton Head Island, S.C.
*Islander*, September, 1972, Hilton Head Island, S.C.

# Boogie Board Surfer
## Thirty Years Later, Oregon Coast

We have a family Seal Club for those who brave
the frigid waters of the Pacific on the Oregon Coast,
and I am about to join.  At eighty-five, my mother
gained admittance when she was barefoot on the beach
and accidentally lost her balance in the sand.
When a wave crept up over her toes, she tumbled over
and became a bit wet.  She wasn't hurt, and snap shots
taken immediately afterward show her looking radiant
and much younger than usual.  Our son and
two granddaughters are hardier than most and
sometimes go in without a wetsuit.  The oldest
granddaughter Anna has to be coaxed or made to
come to shore after as much as an hour in the waves.
Of course, I've wet my toes in the Oregon surf
and done brief bits of wading, but now I am about
to embark on the real thing.

I struggle into my grandson's black wetsuit with
turquoise markings and find it actually fits,
in spite of Julian's greater height and larger shoulders.
I don the boots and, almost despairing of success,
drag the skintight hood over my head, stuffing
my long hair into it, finally managing to free my face.

I draw on the gloves and slip on my hip-length red
raincoat with the hood over the wetsuit. "Are you going to
wear your *raincoat*?" my husband says in disbelief.

"Aren't you afraid you're going to look kind of funny?"
(It's clear he thinks I already do.) "What do I care?" I say.
"I'm not out to look cool or impress anybody. I'm going
to try something new and have an adventure. That wind
is chilly. I'm trying to conserve my body heat." I zip up
the raincoat, pull the hood over my head and put
my wrist through the Boogie Board strap. I carry the
board down the steep hill from Jean's house, walking
beside my son and grandson, down the wooden steps
and out across the wide expanse of Cannon Beach.
We establish a headquarters by a big driftwood log back
in the soft sand a suitable distance south of towering
Haystack Rock and the other black rocks around it.
I tuck my raincoat into the base of the log. Carrying our
boards, my son and I walk toward the white breaking
edges of the Pacific, which looks terribly cold. "This is a
good place to surf," he says. "It's shallow a long way out.
We often come here. But don't let the wind carry you
toward those rocks." He points. "Don't worry. I won't."
My grandson watches with interest.

My son steps into the surf. Taking a deep breath, I
follow gingerly with my soft padded black boots. The
water feels quite cool, but not as cold as I had imagined.
"The wetsuit keeps your body heat in," Jamey says.
The Boogie Board is light blue and shorter than the red
and white air mattress. The technique of catching the
ride is different, a little trickier to master.

We wade out, standing hip to waist deep, sides to the
shore, watching the waves coming in. "You try to judge
which one is going to have the most power," Jamey says,
"then just before it hits, you get up on the board
and lay on your stomach like this, facing the beach,
ready to paddle." He hops on, catches a wave and takes
a short ride, but not all the way in. Looking out to sea,
the swells appear bigger then they turn out to be. It's not
easy to judge their strength. I make several wrong
assessments, plopping stomach down on the Boogie
Board, only to have a froth of white break ineffectually
beneath me, taking me nowhere.

Jamey catches a good one and goes zooming
into the beach. I make a few more tries.
There, the water thunders down just behind my heels.
That's it! Grip the Boogie Board, go.
Shooting shoreward,
down and forward,
skimming smooth water, ahead of the wave,
almost like flight,
so fast, so light,
powered with a dynamo under my knees
and under my thighs,
a tremendous thrust I can't see,
shooting me past startled swimmers
gaping with heads swivelling as I go hurtling by.

My face skims level toward the fast-approaching
beach. I'm on a collision course.
Immediately, I feel its friction.
I plow into the sand.

I'm beached. I'm beached,
no longer sea-borne, but beached,
once more a creature of land.

1998, Cannon Beach, Oreg.

# *Drying My Hair in the Desert*

I sit on the balcony and dry my hair,
the sun warm on my back, the air still,
palm fronds still.  Distant talk of golfers,
a twittering behind me of a bird,
the barely heard roar of a jet far above.
Thankfully, the woman on the terrace below me
has stopped her loud talking on the cell phone
(to her nearly deaf mother.  I heard every word
and identified.  She switched it off.)
Even the Road Runner isn't squawking
from atop the post as he did a while ago.
I hear a clear call, a chirrup.  A door shuts.
Peace.
I feel sleepy.  I will sleep.

February 8, 2002, Palm Desert, Calif.

# *Creating*

When I am creating, I tap a vast source of energy.
I cannot create from myself and my knowledge.
I must be plugged into this energy,
tuned in to its frequency, turned on by its force.
It is related to the natural laws and natural forces which
govern the universe. It often finds expression
in the symbols and sounds of art, music and writing,
in the sudden insight of solving a problem,
in discovery and invention.

I think this energy enters through the unconscious mind,
sometimes through our dreams and daydreams.
It filters through the deepest parts of our being,
using all of our experience and knowledge
as the material for creativity. This energy puts us in awe.
Can we doubt that it comes directly from the Creator
of the universe? No, the energy for creating must come,
in my view, directly from the Creator, from God himself.
That doesn't mean he's dictating, though. It doesn't
mean the words themselves come from him.

Sometimes I think praying is tuning in to God, getting on
his frequency. If we find the right frequency,
his frequency, we can receive his signals for what
he wants us to do. We can tune in and listen by an act of
will. The signals and energy come from him.

Responding to the signals is up to us.

We humans are known to make mistakes
in interpretation and response.  Often
our mistakes are grave ones.
Keep tuning in.  It's mysterious.  And mighty.

1974, SW Mo.

## *Divine Order*

When lives unfold in beauty and
harmony like Lotus flowers,
according to the right time and season,
that is Divine Order.

Spring, 2002, SW Mo.

## *Treasure at Hilton Head*

Beach combing, I found a broken piece of dark brown
glass. "This will cut someone's bare foot," I thought.
"The thing to do is pick it up and throw it way back there
among the sea oats where no one will be walking."
I glanced from water's edge where I was standing,
across the width of wet, hard-packed beach,
beyond the loose white sand to the place where
the tall golden sea oats were bending in the breeze,
with a few green succulents beneath them on
the sand. I picked up the jagged piece of dark glass
and started to walk the fifty yards or so, my eyes
on the deposit each wave had left along the beach.

"Perhaps I'll find some lovely little treasure as a reward,"
I thought. I pictured finding some perfect little gem
of a sea shell, some shining little object from the sea,
unique and rare. I looked eagerly as I walked among
the curving lines of shells, seaweed, debris, for I believe
in miracles large and small. (Only I don't think they are
actually miracles. There is always a cause, a reason.)
I thought I would discover something fine
somewhere upon the sand.

I left the hard, moist beach, walked into warm, loose sand
past old driftwood and cocoanut palm logs and
finally flung the treacherous glass as far as possible,
back among the sea oats, where there was no path.

"Wonder why I didn't find anything?" I thought.
Giving up, I raised my eyes to the ravishing splendor of
the sunset, glowing with golden fire beyond the
blue-gray clouds. I saw it with startled joy, for I had
been oblivious to the sinking of the sun as I walked
northeast up the beach. My trip to throw the broken glass
away had left me facing west, where I could and did look
up and enjoy the priceless treasure
there for the taking and seeing.

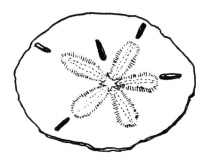

*Islander*, October, 1971, Hilton Head Island, S.C.

## *Pieces of Places*

My husband brings a stone from every favorite place,
for he is a  Stone Man still, even though
he's not taking it from the earth,
crushing or sawing it,
polishing and cutting it anymore.

Wherever he goes, a small piece of the very rock
of the earth to hold in his hands, to smooth
between his fingers, is the memento
he wants to bring back.

In the same way, we each want to bring back
a souvenir of frozen life from those
special experiences and places,
something tangible to touch,
to feel the sharp edges, to weigh in the hand,
to say, "That's white," "That's black,"
"That's quartz," something we could bite
and taste if we had a mind to,
a souvenir of life to bring back home.


1993, SW Mo.

# Why Can't They Get Along?

*The following is my effort to get into the mind of a*
*troubled teen struggling to understand his quarreling*
*parents and find the right course in a turbulent home.*


If they love me so much, why can't they get along?
They've given me the the best of food, clothes,
medical care, shelter, education, but they're *not* giving me
what I need the most, a secure, warm and loving home,
two secure, warm and loving parents
who love each other.

Why don't they love each other?
If only I could understand.
I love them both so much,
yet I resent the way they act.
They both can be so selfish about getting
what they want.  Along with all my love for them,
sometimes I feel a little hatred, too, because
they're not providing what I need.

Hey, maybe that's the way *they* feel about each other!
Maybe Dad feels a little bit of hatred for Mom because
she's not providing what he needs.  And vice-versa.
Is love always mixed with hatred?
Have I provided what they need from me?
Should I be expected to provide what
my parents need?  What do they need from me exactly?

Love, respect, obedience, someone to really listen
to them.  When have I ever really listened?

Someone to bring them together.
Me?  Forget it.  That's a laugh.
How could I do it?

I'm not sure I could,
but, well, maybe there *is* something I could do.
I can definitely try listening
to both of them.  That much I can do.

*Prayer*  God, I can't do it alone, and maybe no one
can change things between them,
but I know you can show me the way to try,
and I'll be yours for loving and caring and
listening and providing what they both need from me.

*Power*, July-September, 1970, Christian Youth Publications.

## *Non-Cool Me*

I want to appear serene, strong and cool.
I want to look cool as cool can be.
I want to look cheerful and good-natured.
What's more, I long to be that way,
but I'm touchy, easily hurt, easily enraged.
My Irish temper goes off like a sky rocket
with no prior notice at all, showering sparks, fire,
angry words, tears and raw emotion
to everyone in sight and sound.
My grandpa had a word for it, a tailspin.

I would like to wear the serene face
of the woman I'd like to be, but I'm no good at it.
I don't even wear a serene mask.
I'm just sensitive, hot-tempered me,
and my family knows it far too well.
If I feel the rage, I guess it's good not to keep
it all inside, but why do I feel it?

My trouble is self-consciousness,
self-centeredness and selfishness.
Anyone else have that problem?

*Prayer:* Break me at the point of my self-centeredness,
God, and make me over so that I don't take offense,
so that I don't see words and actions as slights

and injuries, so that rage doesn't rise inside me,
so that I'm filled always with concern
and love for those around me, forgetting
completely about my selfish self.

*Power*, July, 1970, Christian Youth Publications

*(My prayer is still the same, but I have an update on the next page.)*

# *2002 Addendum to Non-Cool Me*

The Irish temper hasn't disappeared,
I'm sorry to say, but it doesn't explode quite as often.
I've learned some daily routines to help. Meditation,
exercise, Yoga, Tai Chi, walks in the country, centering
myself, following my breath for calmness, being with
like-minded people, praying, claiming Divine Order.

Truly, don Miguel Ruiz has given me the best advice
of all in his great book, *The Four Agreements.* To quote
Agreement #2, "DON'T TAKE ANYTHING
PERSONALLY Nothing others do is because of you.
What others say and do is a projection of their own
reality, their own dream. When you are immune to the
opinions and actions of others, you won't be the victim
of needless suffering". And from Agreement #3,
"DON'T MAKE ASSUMPTIONS Find the courage to ask
questions and express what you really want.
Communicate with others as clearly as you can to avoid
misunderstandings, sadness, and drama. " *

I've learned there are bad times to bring things up,
especially between husband and wife. I've learned not to
upset my mother unnecessarily. I'm learning. A bit.

April 14, 2002, SW Mo.

*From the book The Four Agreements © 1997, don Miguel Ruiz.
Reprinted by permission of Amber-Allen Publishing, Inc. P.O. Box
6657, San Rafael, CA 94903. All rights reserved.*

# Getting a Hold on Freedom

Freedom is a terrible risk.
Bondage is so much safer, more secure.
We list all the reasons why we can't possibly do
the things we know in our hearts we should be doing.
Excuses, reasons, crutches, rationalizations,
imagined duties, people who stand in our way, habits,
faults we think we could never change.

*Prayer:* Lord, you know how lazy I am,
how I waste my time, my energy, my strength,
with all sorts of worthless pastimes, but you also know
my potential, much better than I do, I guess.
You know why you made me and what I'm supposed
to do.  Help me find the courage for freedom,
to do my best and try my hardest and be glad about
doing it, even if I don't reach what I imagine to be
my goal.  I've got faith, Lord, that if I can find out
what you want me to do, I will find strength, courage
and guidance from you to get it done.  I'll walk the path
you want me to walk, have whatever kind of success
you want me to have and reach at least one
of a series of goals you want me to reach.


*Power,* Christian Youth Publications, June, 1971

# Addiction to the Rose
## The War of the Roses, Poetry and Prose

Rose growing spans the furthest extremes of poetry
and prose. The poetry of roses is in the unfurling forms
from bud to bloom to blowsy shattering, in the infinite
variety of hue from delicate tints to vivid colors and rich
deep tones, in the heady fragrances like no other, an
aphrodisiac to rose lovers and dedicated addicts like me.

The humblest, most prosaic and back-breaking of tasks
and labor, such as digging, planting, weeding, feeding,
mulching, spraying and dead heading lead to the poetry
of bloom, which is so often chosen to speak the universal
language of love, sympathy and appreciation.

Our climate in Southwest Missouri isn't what roses like
best. It's too humid, too hot, too cold, too windy,
sometimes too dry. Roses much prefer Portland, Oregon,
Seattle, Washington, California, Vancouver or Victoria in
British Columbia, France, Ireland or England.

Now I kneel on the east side of my front walk, by my
round rose bed, digging and pulling out the long roots of
Bermuda Grass from the soil, a nearly impossible task.
Some say the roots can be fifteen or twenty feet long.
I dare not leave one small piece of root or grass in the
soil. I pick the rose leaves marred by Black Spot off the
bushes, careful not to drop a single one on the ground or
to touch healthy leaves with my hands or garden gloves.

Feeling like a surgical nurse, I change them often. Black Spot is a fungus. When I see fallen leaves with dark round spots, I pick them up and put all the Black Spot leaves and rose hips in a plastic trash bag or burn them.

Bermuda Grass and Black Spot, you are the enemies of my beloved roses, and therefore my enemies, too, the bane of my life as a gardener. In that category, I list Aphids, too, for they leave a sticky honey dew which encourages Black Spot. I fight the Aphids with a hard stream of water to knock them off the bushes early in the day, by using soapy sprays with baking soda, or a little systemic insecticide in the soil.

Lola Edwards, my neighbor years ago who raised glorious roses along our fence line in town, taught me to pick off the Black Spot leaves. She did it while we talked. I didn't realize then that she was giving me the best of advice, which she did on other important subjects.

I grow some Climbers and many varieties of Old and Modern Shrub Roses. "Carefree Beauty", developed by Dr. Griffin Buck at Iowa State, is a favorite. I have a huge "Carefree Beauty" on the south in full sun and another on the northwest in the shade. To my surprise, David Austin English Roses do well on our exposed and windy south-facing slope, and less surprisingly, Rugosas and their hybrids. A bed of seven thrives just east of our drive. I grow Bourbons, Meidiland Landscape Roses, Hybrid Musks and Canadian-bred Explorer Series.

Wanting to bring old friends with me to the country, I started the dark red Grandiflora "Carousel" from my old rose bed on Forest Street, as well as four large shrubs of the vigorous, free-blooming Polyantha Rose "The Fairy", named long before the connotations of today. It blooms from late May to frost in charming leafy sprays of dainty small pink flowers and buds that do wonders for fresh bouquets. This spring, my son helped me plant "Red Fairy" and two new Rugosa Hybrids.

Some of the best Floribundas thrive on our high river bluff, but Hybrid Teas languish. I grow only a couple of these sensitive beauties. They are far too temperamental for the harsh conditions at our place, with its strong southwest winds and wide temperature swings. For the rose lover, even the names are poetry. Sweet Juliette, Dublin Bay, Sally Holmes, Linda Campbell, The Pilgrim, Heritage, Tournament of Roses, Sharifa Asthma, Dainty Bess, Jens Munk, Bow Bells. And Freulingsgold, Betty

Prior, Sunsprite, Double Delight, Playboy, Ballerina, Alba, Topaz Jewel, Madame Isaac Pereire, New Dawn, Hansa, Bonica, Roserie de l'Hay, Queen Elizabeth, Blanc Double de Courbet, Chrysler Imperial, Louise Odier, Cecile Brunner. In late winter and spring, I can't resist the terribly addictive drug of pouring over rose catalogs in hopes of finding a place for just one more.

Why is it that Black Spot begins to dot the leaves when the roses are most beautiful and wildly bountiful in May? Don't I test the soil, and feed with Epsom Salts, Rose Food and Fish Emulsion? Don't I spray with dormant oil, baking soda, fungicides and fungicidal soap? The moisture that makes the roses bloom so carelessly prolific also makes the leaves crunchy and delicious for Aphids, helps to cause the dread Black Spot and makes Bermuda Grass thrive to send forth its greedy tentacles and roots. No doubt each has a function to perform in the scheme of things, as does the rose.

It's Nature, simply Nature.

As for my addiction to the rose, I don't believe I'll get over it any time soon. I'm too far gone and fascinated.

July 2002, SW Mo.

# *For My Mother*

Spring flowers from your garden,
Siberian iris, yellow roses,
daisies and delicate white flowers
arranged with care in your crystal bowl
and put on my table for a special party
are symbols of all the loving things
you 've done for me year after year.

My children cared for as we traveled,
clothes mended, fixed, made new,
fresh vegetables and lovely flowers
May to November.

Always coming when we needed you,
always coming up with what I needed,
even an understanding of the Christ,
the Creative thought, principal and
spoken spiritual Word in action.

All this I see as love,
and as I recognize how richly
you've blessed me with love ,
I think we grow closer
together than ever before.
Happy Mother's Day
with love from your daughter.

May, 1969, SW Mo.

## Whence Cometh these Loves?

Is the love of gardening, fishing and cooking
inherited? Is it carried on the chromosomes or
genes? Or is it learned by example, a matter of
the home and environment?

I know my love of growing flowers, herbs, shrubs and
trees comes from both of my grandmothers (the one
I never knew and the one I knew so well), from
my father and from my mother, who became an
enthusiastic gardener in her late forties. Gardening
and working in the soil is therapy for me. I'm not
crazy about fighting voracious insects, though, or
weeding, except on rare occasions when the ground
is soaked and the weeds pull up delightfully well.

For six generations, all the women in my mother's
family and my family have loved to fish.
Not only do we like to catch fish, we like to cook them
and, better yet, eat them. I vividly remember my
Great-Aunt Hettie walking in from a fishing expedition
on her farm in her long print dress, pleated organdy cap
and sunbonnet, with a cane pole over her shoulder,
when she was nearly ninety. Her niece Edna was
carrying their stringer of fish, and both of them
were beaming. "Yes, we had *such* a good time,"
Aunt Hettie said in her surprisingly low-pitched voice.
By that time, she was quite short, but she still retained
a bit of her earlier sturdiness.

Breakfast fish fries with corn bread, sorghum
molasses and fried potatoes were a fond tradition in
the farm home of my grandparents. My first cousin
Charles Jay Hammons carried on the tradition of
breakfast fish fries in the same house as long as he
lived. After his mother died, he loved to invite
his father, sometimes my husband and me, and
always my mother, who was a widow by then.
She and I carried on the fish fry tradition, too.

For me, it was usually at the lake, after a big catch.
My Grandma Hammons was Great-Aunt Hettie's
sister Delie. They were two of the Larcher sisters.
They came from hard-working farm families,
Old German Baptist Brethren, commonly known as
Dunkers or Dunkards. Every family planted a
vegetable garden and orchard, then picked, canned,
dried, pickled and preserved in order to have enough
food to feed the family and survive through the winter.
But some people enjoyed gardening better than others,
and my grandma was one of them.

Sarah Ellen Cromwell Riley was the grandma I never
knew, because she died even before my parents met.
She, too, loved to grow flowers and vegetables.
After she was widowed with a family of boys to support,
she became a cook and housekeeper. Her youngest
son, who would become my father, was only
six years old. And he was always deeply interested in
gardening, vegetables, fruit, food preparation and eating.

He knew how to graft fruit trees and sometimes
kept bees and gathered honey.

My son and daughter are fine gardeners both
and earned their degrees in Botany.
They both love to cook and so do their sons.
One of those boys is growing tomatoes and herbs now.

Whether from example, environment or genes,
these loves don't stop.  They go down the generations
one by one, bred in our bones, our hands, our brains,
our very souls.

August-September, 2002, SW Mo.

Jay and me fishing at the pond closest to the farmhouse, about 1945.

# Spring River Saga

*Now there is no one left who remembers family events during my childhood and teen years except my mother and me. She is ninety-nine, completed her memoirs not long ago, and I am writing this book.*

*No one else now living remembers or ever knew what it was like for our family during the time we spent on the Spring River farm.*

*In "Spring River Saga", I write in the vein of nostalgia and storytelling as I recall a certain place and certain people who shaped my life.*

*During our New York City years, my parents and I always spent our summers on the Spring River farm back home in Southwest Missouri. We seldom returned to the city until October, and wasn't I the lucky child to be able to go with my cousin Jay to his one-room school near Spring River whenever I wanted to, which was most of the time? We carried our tin lunch boxes, walking all the way in good weather, played softball and tag or Hide-and-Seek at recess, used the "privies" out back and helped sweep out the schoolhouse when asked, in stark contrast to my life at school in Manhattan.*

*In early October, Mother and Daddy and I left by train, with its sleeping cars and elegant dining car, ready to walk a little faster on the streets of New York City, breathing deeply of its brisk salt air. The energy was contagious, and we all enjoyed it.*

*I knew the best of both worlds, or thought I did, and plunged into both of them with relish.*

*There was a time when authors felt free to address their readers, and now I am going to do the same. As early novelists used to write, "bear with me if you will, dear reader" as I share these memories of what life was like for me in my grandparents' home and on their farm.*

## *Delie*, The Grandma I Knew

She could be so much fun, joking and laughing in great
explosive whoops with my cousin Jay and me, with
Jay's dad Paul or my father Perry, the son-in-law who
was always teasing her, to her great delight. Daddy
and Mother and I lived in Grandma and Grandpa's
home for a total of three and a half years of my life.
Long summers in my childhood and two winters
when I was older, in high school and college.

I slept with her when I was a child, inside in winter
or bad weather, outside on the upstairs sleeping porch
in summer, listening to the hoot owls, whippoorwills,
peepers, bullfrogs and cicadas, which we called katydids.
There, we pulled the homemade quilt up to our chins and
slept on a comfortable mattress over open coil springs.
When we first went to bed, we talked and laughed.
At last we were quiet, listened to the night sounds and
fell asleep. In the middle of the night, it usually became
so cool Grandma would cover us with an old knotted
comforter made by her family, soft gray wool on one side.

When I woke up in the morning, Grandma was always
up, dressed and downstairs cooking or eating breakfast.
I could hear everyone talking and laughing from the
screened porch just below me, where Grandma kept a big
table at one end. The family often ate on that porch in
warm weather. I could hear the skeptical hoots of
laughter from my Uncle Paul, the way he whistled

Sarah Adelia Larcher Hammons
May 30, 1881 to July 28, 1976

as he walked off toward his chores and farm work. I
could hear Grandma stomping about the house with her
heavy walk, humming or singing hymns in her high-
pitched nasal voice. I learned to play "There's a Church
in the Valley by the Wildwood" on the piano, and when
I played it, we would sing the old hymn together.

Grandma's favorite chair was a heavy oak rocker with
a wide seat and large curved arms. It was only a few
steps into the living room from the dining room table
and was angled to carry on conversations with anyone
still at the dining table or anywhere in the living room
and also to face the fireplace. Grandma would rest there
after meals and I would snuggle down in her lap or

sit by her side as we talked and rocked together.

Nothing could have been more comfortable and pleasant
to me than rocking with Grandma as I grew so drowsy
I sometimes fell asleep, and so did she. I remember
the sweet-smelling breeze that came through
the window nearby on warm balmy afternoons.

She was the grandmother I knew and loved.

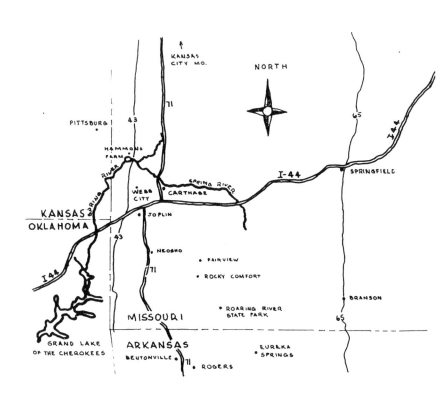

2005 map showing Spring River Saga locations.

## *Early Days*

In 1889, when Delie was eight years old, she traveled west
in a covered wagon with her parents, brothers and sisters.
They would establish a farm home in Southwest Missouri
near Fairview in Newton County, southeast of Neosho.
That's where, on a neighboring farm, she would meet her
future husband, Andrew Dolison Hammons, known
throughout his life as Dolly or A.D.

Delie was born near Dayton, Ohio, on May 30, 1881,
into a Pennsylvania Dutch farming family of second and
third generation Americans. Their ancestors originated
from a village near Bern, Switzerland and from both sides
of the Rhine. Long before there was a Germany, her
people had sailed from Rotterdam with other like-minded
families to cross the Atlantic in search of a better life with

religious freedom. As I mentioned in *Whence Cometh These Loves?* (p. 115), Delie's father and mother were thrifty hard-working Old Order German Baptist Brethren, a group often called Dunkards or Dunkers because they baptized by immersion. Those who belonged to the Church wore a "habit" similar to the Amish and Mennonites.

English was Delie's second language. She did not learn to speak, read or write English until first grade. Grandma was brought up "plain", but never joined the church of her family or assumed the "habit." She didn't marry until she was twenty-three, because she "was having too much fun with the boys," she used to say, her eyes lively and bright with remembrance. "They like to tease me." I imagine her "too much fun" was fairly innocent, by today's standards.

Family legend has it that she was also older than usual in marrying because it required some time for my grandfather to soften up her parents with fine black leather shoes and beautiful black fabrics he brought back to them from St. Louis for their plain Dunker attire. It was all part of his extended sales campaign to win Delie's hand in marriage. He was operating a mercantile store in the nearby town of Rocky Comfort and made buying trips to St. Louis. Mercantile stores, which were later called general stores, stocked everything from plows, animal feed, seed, tools and hardware to staple food, barrels of pickles and dried fish, slabs of bacon, thick squares of tobacco, overalls, fabrics, thread, needles and ribbons, shotgun shells and shoes.

A.D. told Delie's parents he loved her and promised that if they married, she could always go to any church she wished and take their children with her. His strategy worked. It was also a promise he kept. A.D. and Delie were married on March 6, 1904, and set up housekeeping in Rocky Comfort. She was the only one of the four Larcher sisters allowed to marry outside the family church. In spite of the triumph of marrying the man she

1912-1914, Eureka Springs, Ark. From right, Maggie Green Estes, owner of the horse and surrey, her son Orville, Grandma and children Juanita, Paul and Lorraine (my mother), and Grandpa.

Front row, l., my grandfather Andrew Dolison Hammons, oldest of his brothers, all shown with their father William T., front center.

loved, she could not escape being deeply influenced by the way she had been raised and experienced many inner conflicts throughout most of her life.

Grandpa's family was Baptist, too, but of the more Southern pioneer variety. His family had moved west from Virginia, the Carolinas and Georgia through Tennessee to Arkansas and Missouri and included spunky, feisty pioneer women ready to defend their families from all comers. The men served and fought, however reluctantly, in every war in our nation's history, beginning with the War for Independence.

A.D. and Delie's two daughters were born in Rocky
Comfort, but within a few years, A.D. moved the
household back to Fairview, close to both their families.
Grandpa opened his Fairview Mercantile Company store
before the birth of their son and youngest child in 1908.

Grandma's lively conversation was always peppered with
Pennsylvania Dutch phrases, words and expressions,
when she couldn't call the English ones to mind. To her
children and grandchildren, it seemed a back-to-front

Grandpa, Grandma and children on lawn of their Fairview, Mo.
home, about 1916. Mother is the little girl standing at left.

Inside Grandpa's mercantile store, Fairview, Mo., 1915-1919

or upside-down way of putting things, often puzzling, sometimes bringing a smile, but always fascinating, distinctive, and to her grandchildren at least, endearing. If she said she was feeling *schussli*, we gathered she was feeling a bit scatterbrained, disorganized and clumsy. Maybe out of sorts and ill at ease or "antsy" as we might say today. She often used the prefix *ker*. Somebody fell in the water "kerplunk." Or an object might be slammed down "kerplunk." If he went down "kerflummox," he fell down hard in the most embarrassing way. Or, he lost his credibility to the point where in today's parlance, he "crashed and burned."

I am sorry to admit that by their own accounts my aunt and my mother were a little ashamed of Grandma and her ways of speaking and dressing when they were "thoroughly modern" flappers with bobbed hair in their late teens and early twenties. I don't know how their brother felt. As the years went by, of course, the two sisters mellowed and became more amused, fonder and much more tolerant of their mother.

1912-1914, Eureka Springs, Ark. My grandparents Delie and A.D. with Juanita, above, Paul and Lorraine (my mother), wearing a hat.

## The Farm on Spring River

Once in the second decade of the Twentieth Century,
the Spring River farm was called "Blairs Lea." It was
used as an experimental model farm by the Agricultural
Editor of *The Joplin Globe* newspaper. In 1919, Grandpa
changed professions and assumed a large mortgage to
acquire it. He bought three hundred and sixty-five
acres of rich bottom land bordering Spring River north
of Joplin, Missouri. A two-story white farmhouse, large
barn and outbuildings stood on a hill overlooking the
fields and pastures, which were underlaid with clay
drainage pipes. Groves of pecans grew in the pastures

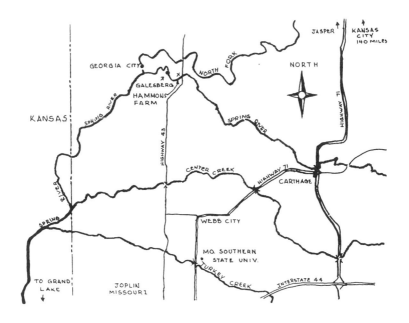

2005 map showing Spring River, the farm, towns past and present.

and black walnut trees and oaks near the house and barn.
Woodlands fringed the cultivated land and the river,
which could not be seen from the house except in flood
stage. The farm was studded with a lake and ponds
teaming with fish.

"A perfect place to raise my son," Grandpa thought.
The boy was about ten then and subject to bad influences,
Grandpa believed, in the small town of Fairview, in
Newton County, where Grandpa had been running his
mercantile store, Ford dealership and garage. He sold
Ford Model T's and tractors, sharing the profits with his
uncle, who had brought some gold home from Alaska
and invested it to help Grandpa open the Ford agency.

Winter snow scene showing back of barn and outbuildings, 1925.

At the Spring River farm, a windmill pumped water into
storage tanks and powered a generator called the Delco,
which supplied some weak and intermittent electric
power to the house. Inside was the miracle of indoor
plumbing, as rare as electricity in country homes in 1919.
The farm was only a half mile west of Highway 43, along
a secondary road. A second small yellow frame house
stood on the property near the road, and there was an
office between the main house and the barn.

Only one looming feature marred what Grandpa
regarded as the near perfection of the farm. It was the
*Missouri Pacific Railroad* track and embankment between
the road and the house. With this hump running
roughly parallel to the road came dangers, advantages
and disadvantages. Fires could start along the track, but
*Missouri Pacific* workers kept it clear of weeds and brush,
and it was a good place to pick blackberries. Children
had to be taught to get off the tracks to one side the

moment they heard the loud warning whistle. In periods of heavy rain, the raised embankment was usually well above water, providing easy access to other parts of the farm.

The house, with its red brick chimney and large screened porches could be seen in the distance the moment one turned south into the farm lane from the road and drove across the cattle guard. The lane divided a pasture, then rose by a good deep pond to cross the *Missouri Pacific* grade, where one had a splendid view of the entire layout of farmhouse and yard, windmill, towering barn roof and outbuildings.

Grandpa moved his family of a wife, son and two daughters one county north to his new farm close to the Kansas/Missouri line. The nearest community was Galesburg just to the west, where his son and youngest daughter walked to school along the railroad track.

My mother Lorraine with big bow, Juanita and Paul, right. All three siblings were musical. Grandma taught the sisters to sing harmony for church duets when Lorraine was three.

On Sundays, community worship was held in the Galesburg schoolhouse.

The Galesburg picnic was where my mother and father first got together in 1924. Lorraine was A.D. and Delie's youngest daughter and by that time, she was seventeen and a student at Webb City High School. Perry Riley had noticed her slim figure and smooth cap of dark "bobbed" hair as he was driving along Highway 43 and she was removing the family mail from a rural mailbox on the west side of the highway. She received a courteous and charming note from him, asking if he could meet her. Her sister Juanita, a little more than two years older than Lorraine, protested indignantly that there must be some

Mother on the running board of Daddy's car about 1927-1928.

Uncle Paul and Grandpa at the farm. Barn in background.

Picnic in the front yard at Spring River Farm, about 1941.
From left, Grandpa, Grandma, Daddy and Mother.

mistake, that he must have intended the letter for her.
My grandfather made some inquiries about Perry Riley
and decided he would be willing to greet and appraise
this twenty-nine year old bachelor from Georgia City, if
he came to call upon Lorraine.

In the meantime, Perry decided to go to the Galesburg
picnic, hoping to see Lorraine there. She decided to take
a scratch angel food cake and began separating the yolks
from the whites of a dozen fresh eggs and beating the
whites into snowy peeks by hand. Later, at the picnic,
a few bites of that light and tender angel food cake
finished off the job of winning Perry Riley's heart
completely. And as soon as Lorraine's family began to
know him, they loved him like a son and brother. It was
lucky for him, as he had no family of his own by then,
except a much older brother in western Kansas.

Standing from left, Grandma's mother Esther Miller Larcher, 80,
Grandma and Mother seated, holding me, 1931 on the farm.

In photos of the 1920s, the yard and the barnyard look
neat and bare, but when I first remember the place about
1933 or 1934, climbing roses grew on the fence near the
railroad track, as well as a row of flowering shrubs--
lilacs, forsythia, a snowball bush and spirea. Iris,
daffodils, tulips and daylilies bordered the drive.
I remember when it was made into a circle drive.
Grandma grew cannas, roses, zinnias and mums in the
oval flower bed in the center. Sometimes she mowed
the huge lawn herself with an old-fashioned rotary
push mower. She always tied a print sunbonnet under
her chin on sunny days when she worked outdoors.

Juanita and Lorraine were ambitious and embarked
on careers, Juanita in business, Lorraine as a singer.

Grandpa and Grandma were proud of them and usually
encouraging. The farm and its buildings expanded as
the family bought more acreage and built a new house
for Paul, Inah and Jay. Inah's father John Crocker erected
a clubhouse at the lake for fishing and parties. Paul
and his son Jay never wanted to live anywhere else and
worked on the land all their lives, except when Jay
enlisted in the U.S. Army Air Force during the
Korean War.

The farm would become a beloved home, spiritual center
and refuge for four generations of the Hammons family.
Grandpa would have been glad to know the close
neighbors to the east along the river were the ones who
bought the farm after Jay and Paul were gone.

Picnic at the farm lake. From left, Aunt Inah, Grandpa, Jay, Uncle
Paul, Daddy, Grandma and myself on blanket, 1939-1940.

## *The Front Porch Swing*

Besides the screened porches, one above the other,
there was another porch at Grandpa and Grandma's
house. It was the front porch, a wonderful open porch
facing southwest and looking out across the fields and
pastures of the valley toward the thick line of trees
bordering the lake and Spring River just beyond.
White wooden columns supported the overhanging
roof. On the porch was a swing big enough for two or
three to sit side by side and a footrest that could be
used to pump the swing higher. Even on the hottest of

summer days, it was by far the coolest place to be. Tall
black walnut trees, hickories and oaks with shiny green
leaves provided welcome shade. There was always a
bit of breeze, however faint. Some of the happiest times
of my early life were spent on that swing with Grandma,
my cousin Jay and with other members of the family.

At the bottom of the hill before us was the farm lane,
the vegetable garden and beyond it, we could glimpse
the progress of work in the fields and pastures, the farm
equipment, horses, cattle, people and vehicles. A large
dinner bell hung near the porch steps to summon the
men from the fields, if only we could ring it loudly
enough to attract their attention. Below us to our left
was a fenced area containing the orchard, henhouse and
rabbit warren and, in the shade to our right, the sandpile,
where Jay and I dug our toes into the cool sand and spent

Grandma with Jay and me, her only grandchildren, at the farm.

delightful hours building castles, moats and forts. He was good at sound effects as we enacted long scenarios with his toy trucks and cars, soldiers, horses, cowboys and Indians, all within view of the front porch swing.

I should explain that whenever Daddy, Mother and I arrived at the farm for an extended visit, I was expected to pitch in the very next day to help with all the chores, inside and outside the house. This meant doing whatever Grandma or any of the adults asked me to do and sharing Jay's regular morning and evening duties of gathering eggs and feeding and watering the chickens, rabbits and some other animals. For me, fresh from apartment or hotel living in New York cities, it was fun, and I never minded the work in the slightest. Milking, though, was a skill I never mastered. The cows and I were all too nervous.

Mother and I leave Macy's Thanksgiving Parade, N.Y. City, 1940.

Grandma kneels to watch as Jay (left) and I (right) play with his trucks in the sand pile. View of fields at bottom of hill behind her.

Grandma and I often sat together on the porch swing with newspapers or paper sacks on our laps, with a kettle or large bowl between us, stemming and slicing strawberries, pitting red cherries and peeling apples or peaches. We peeled potatoes, raw or cooked in their skins for potato salad, shelled peas, cut the eyes out of new potatoes and chunked them up, sometimes to cook with the peas, snapped green beans, and peeled carrots, onions and cucumbers. My favorite of all was peeling cold boiled beets. I loved the way the skins slipped right off so easily. We would peel hard-boiled eggs, too, for deviled eggs, potato salad and one other important use. Grandma knew how to make delicious pickled beets, and she would often use a quart jar to alternate beets with the hard boiled eggs, which became rosy and well-seasoned from the pickled beet juice. As we worked, we always had a great time visiting and talking.

It was on the front porch swing with Grandma and in her small kitchen that I first became interested in food preparation and started to learn about cooking. I became actively involved in the work of canning and pickling that went on all summer and fall. I helped to can apples and applesauce, peaches, cherries, green beans, corn, tomatoes and all kinds of pickles, including a delicious relish called "Last of the Garden." I loved Grandma's dill pickles with a passion and after I was grown, Mother would teach me to make them myself.

Grandma even canned chunks of beef. When she opened the jar later, she could fry the beef, cook it with noodles or dumplings or make a stew with vegetables. Every way was good. She taught me how to churn butter and make cottage cheese, which she drained in a muslin bag from the clothes line outdoors, before breaking it up with a fork and adding cream, milk and a little salt.

During World War II, we bought white margarine sealed in plastic bags with a spot of yellow food coloring, and the front porch swing was a good place to sit while kneading the bag to work and distribute the yellow color uniformly all through the margarine to make it look like butter. By that time, Grandpa and Uncle Paul were raising Hereford beef cattle on a big scale, a far more profitable operation which eventually allowed them to pay off Grandpa's 1919 mortgage. Some of the cattle had complete pedigrees, and a few of the bulls

were registered. I don't remember whether Grandpa
and Paul had stopped keeping milk cows altogether by
that time or if most of the cream was sold to make butter
and cheese for the armed forces.

I do remember that during World War II, the front
porch swing was a good place to paste sugar stamps
into ration books and try to figure out if any of us had
enough left for buying sugar to make jam, jelly, ice
cream, applesauce, or desserts. Like the whole country,
we also needed ration stamps for butter, margarine and
any kind of meat we wanted to buy, even hot dogs,
bacon or lunch meat. Beef or pork took more stamps

My cousin Jay with his dog and rifle, railroad track in background.

than lamb, poultry, fish or seafood. The men took care of pasting in the precious gasoline and oil stamps, but the females studied dress patterns in the swing and tried to decide how many print feed sacks it would take to make a skirt, dress, smock or apron in a certain size. Deals were made among us as we traded favorite prints and colors. Aunt Inah made it fun. The important thing was knowing exactly what kind and color of feed sacks to buy next time we went to the feed store in the small towns of Neck City, Oronogo, Alba, Purcell or Webb City. The feed sacks were not burlap but substantial cotton woven tightly enough to retain the feed within. I remember how hard it was to decide between the many appealing patterns and colors available and come up with the right number of sacks to make the desired

Mother and Daddy, New York City, 1940.

garment. Mother and Aunt Inah did the sewing on their machines. Mother had her own electric Singer machine at the farm and Grandma had an old-fashioned treadle sewing machine, which I would sometimes attempt to use. Unsuccessfully, most of the time. Silk stockings were almost unobtainable, and nylons had not yet come on the market. Women could buy thick cotton stockings, which were warm but not pretty at all, in flesh-colored tones. In summer, we tanned or used leg makeup, even painting on darker lines down the backs of our calves to look like the seams of silk stockings. I was doing this by the time I was in the eighth grade, along with a good part of the other young females in the U.S.

We all knew our country was in a fight for survival. We had to make do with what we had. If we couldn't get much sugar, butter or silk, we could improvise with corn syrup, honey, saccharin, molasses, margarine, rayon and feed sack fabrics.

Those excursions to buy groceries and farm supplies were great adventures for me when I was younger. The smallest towns closest to the farm were all former lead and zinc mining towns. Tiny, but tough. I loved to split a lime or orange popsickle with Jay or pick a frigid cream soda bottle out of the ice in the cooler. We delighted in spending our pocket money on crackers called Guess Whats and couldn't wait to pop them open immediately to discover our paper hats, pieces of candy and prizes, such as a tiny toy, game or magic trick.

If there was time, the adults let us to go to the skating rink, where Jay always roller skated far better than I did, and big rough-looking boys asked me to skate. Once in awhile I agreed, since it was much easier for me to stay upright around the rink in cross-hands position with one of them. Someone in the family was usually in the stands keeping an eye on us, which was a good thing in view of how tough some of those adolescent boys looked.

My father pushing me in old-time wheelbarrow, March, 1937

My grandparents A.D. and Delie with her parents the Larchers,
Harris, Kansas, 1925.

## *Grandma's Cooking*

Delie's good old-fashioned farm cooking was strongly
influenced by the Pennsylvania Dutch cooking of her
mother's kitchen. She stewed beef or chicken with
homemade noodles or dumplings, often fixed potato
soup with egg "rivelings" for supper, and relied heavily
on apples, cabbage, beets, pickles and all sorts of
homegrown fruits and vegetables.

She helped the men in making sausage and curing hams
and bacon, and was well-known for her fruit and
meringue pies, fried chicken with mashed potatoes and
cream gravy and especially for her sliced cold pressed
chicken, my all-time favorite. (See recipe.) Her baked
chicken with dressing was great, too. Of course,

she raised the chickens herself and cooked them immediately after wringing their necks in two seconds, chopping off their heads with an axe, scalding, picking off their feathers, cleaning and dressing them.

In the winter, a quarter of beef was hung on the upstairs sleeping porch, where it stayed ice cold or frozen. Grandma would sometimes slice off steak to pound, dip in flour and fry for breakfast, to serve with eggs and cream gravy made from the scrapings in the bottom of the cast iron skillet. If there was leftover pie, she might offer that for breakfast, too. She usually cooked oatmeal for Grandpa and the family. Whatever was left, he finished off in the evening, eaten cold with cream and a heap of white sugar. Sometimes, she baked muffins, biscuits or made a double batch of white cornmeal mush. After breakfast, she poured the leftover mush into a deep oblong glass dish to chill overnight in the ice box, sometimes adding pork cracklings or bacon. Next morning, she cut it into slices, fried it golden and served it hot with syrup or honey. (See Grandma's Recipes.)

Supper was a light meal, after the large dinner she served at noon. Perhaps Grandma would make soup and set out pickles, bread, butter, homemade apple butter or applesauce and molasses. Anything in addition to that was strictly everyone for himself, foraging for leftovers in the ice box or making sandwiches. If Grandpa could find cornbread leftover from breakfast or dinner, he loved to crumble it up in a bowl and eat cornbread and milk.

I loved both of these dresses. Mother made my navy and white checked taffeta dress in our Manhattan apartment by hand and with my child's manual crank Singer machine. During summers on the farm, she altered family garments on her electric Singer sewing machine and made new clothes for me and Grandma.

# Stormy Nights at the Farm

Doing anything with Grandma was exciting for me,
even during violent after-midnight thunderstorms when
she insisted everyone in the house had to get up, get
dressed and come downstairs into the living room to wait
it out, with kerosene lanterns fully lit. The dim electric
lights from the generator were apt to fail at these times.

Grandma was terrified of storms, wind, hail, the
lightning that could be so fierce on that hill with its tall
trees, the threat of tornados which might roar out of
Kansas, of floods and drowning. Once she had been in a
house when it was struck by lightning. She became
agitated and relived it every time she told us about seeing
a ball of fire come down one corner of the room and leap
to the other side, how she felt the hairs rise on her head.
Even Mother had seen such a thing. No doubt, any of us
would have been marked by such an experience.

Though I grumbled about being wakened from a sound
sleep to get out of bed and put on my clothes, though I
flinched at the bolts of lightning hitting close by,
followed so soon by menacing roars of thunder, I must
confess that once I was downstairs, I was caught up by
the novelty and excitement of the bizarre scene in the
shadowy living room. Even when I was little, I followed
my father's lead in venturing out under the cover of the
front porch roof to observe the storm more closely,
to feel the cool wind and moisture in our faces and

gratefully inhale the fresh smell of rain until Mother or Grandma would demand that we come back inside.

Daddy always had a grin and a quip to try to tease and distract Delie, as he called her, from her panic and terror, if only for a moment, and if my irreverent Uncle Paul and Aunt Inah were there from next door, they did, too. My cousin Jay, three and a half years younger than I, would be with them, making it a party. Even though Grandma's fear didn't go away, she enjoyed the teasing of Paul and my dad Perry, and would soon be answering them right back. To me, those stormy nights were a lark and a thrill.

If the wind came up high enough and the tree limbs began to bend and whip around or start to snap, or if there was a sudden eerie calm in the midst of the storm, threatening a tornado, Grandma would say, "We've got to go to the cellar." The door was right between the living room and the kitchen, and the moment someone opened the door and turned on the bulb hanging over the wooden steps, a musty unmistakable smell of the earth itself would assail us. There was a crude wooden railing on one side and the cool rock and concrete on the other as we descended past rows of canned food in glass jars to the hard-packed dirt floor of the cellar, where potatoes or apples were usually laid out until ready to use. The big coal furnace was down there, too, and some coal at the bottom of the chute.

Grandma was one of the most complex characters I have ever known, undoubtedly neurotic, full of conflicts and contradictions, mostly concerned with religion and standards of right and wrong, a woman who liked to stay home on the farm, who suffered from debilitating migraine headaches and was often reclusive. I vividly remember her coming out of the house to get in the car many times, dressed to go somewhere, with all the rest of us ready to go, too. Grandma would look at the sky, and if she saw clouds, she might say, "I'm afraid it's going to rain. I believe I'll just stay home." Then she'd turn and go back in the farmhouse, leaving the rest of the family to decide what we were going to do. If we cancelled the outing, I usually felt quite disappointed. If we did decide to go, it wasn't as much fun without her.

She and my grandfather loved and adored each other. Though he liked to go places and see people much better than she did, he was unfailingly indulgent with her whims, fears and foibles, which he knew so well. He would just shrug and grin as the screen door slammed behind her, raise his palms up and say, "Well, that's Delie!"

Why did I love Grandma so much, in spite of everything? I can't explain it, really. All I know is that nearly everything about her was precious to me.
And I loved Grandpa just as much.

# *Washing Grandma's Hair*

Once when I was about ten or eleven, Daddy and
Mother were shopping in town.  Grandma wanted to
wash her long hair in rain water, the way she always did,
and I volunteered to help.  Incidentally, her hair hung to
her waist in back, though it was not particularly thick.
We had to heat part of the rain water in the tea kettle
and somehow get the temperature just right.

We were in the kitchen, and the shampooing itself went
well enough.  But when her head was down and I was
rinsing her hair, I managed to get it in a terrible snarl.
I dried it off, worked and worked on the impossible

Grandma, center, with two of her sisters, Hettie Larcher, left, and
Bertha Larcher Miller, right, on the Spring River Farm.

tangles, and we finally decided there was no help for it but to get the scissors out and try to cut through the worst of it. Grandma was a good sport about the whole thing, and the two of us laughed a lot during our debacle. I was a bit panicky as to what Mother would have to say when she got home. Grandma and I both thought we should have the problem mostly solved before Mother returned or we would be in big trouble with her. We managed to get Grandma's hair dried off and the worst of the tangles out before Daddy and Mother drove up to the back door.

Of course, Mother said we should never have attempted such a thing and scolded us both a bit, especially me. But then, she took the scissors and trimmed up Grandma's hair as best she could. We finished drying it, and Mother braided it and crossed the braids on top of Grandma's head like a coronet in the becoming style she had invented. I was saved, and I think Grandma thought she was, too.

Neither of us ever forgot it.

Grandma and Grandpa are the figures at the right in this photo of threshing grain in a field at the Spring River Farm, 1920-1928.

## *Harvest Time*

All men, women and children on the farm were expected to pitch in and work hard when harvest time came.  In early days, the threshing crew was made up of family, neighbors and two or three "hired hands." As time went on, Grandpa and Paul bought a combine, which they used for several years, but it required extra workers, too.

If any of the farm equipment or trucks broke down, and something usually did, Grandpa called for Daddy, who had a talent for figuring out what was wrong and getting vehicles and machinery operating again.  He could fix almost anything around the farm, especially anything electrical, and that included the Delco. Grandpa and Uncle Paul depended on Daddy and Aunt Inah as drivers and gofers. They drove empty and loaded grain trucks back and forth to the fields or sped into town for emergency supplies, tools and repair parts.

Years later, Grandpa and Paul hired a combining crew who brought in their own heavy farm machinery and traveled from farm to farm as the grain ripened.

Cooking for threshers or the combining crew, was a major undertaking in which all the females and children on the farm took part. Grandma, Aunt Inah and Mother cooked wonderful midday meals for the harvesters. Often they served fried chicken, mashed potatoes, cream gravy, cooked fresh vegetables, cole slaw, sliced tomatoes, cucumbers with onions, biscuits or rolls and fresh baked pies. Sometimes they cooked pot roast with vegetables or beef with noodles or dumplings. The men drank plenty of iced tea, water and coffee.

Grandma always set an attractive table in the dining room with a white linen cloth and silver plated flatware. Once the tablecloth was on, I helped set the table for the right number of diners and Grandma sent me out in the yard with a pair of scissors to pick a few flowers and arrange them for a small centerpiece. That done, Grandma or Mother might tell me to slice tomatoes and arrange them on a small platter or peel and slice

My grandfather Andrew Dolison Hammons, 1879 to 1952.

cucumbers and put them in a bowl with ice and salt.
When the men came from the fields in trucks, they
washed their hands and faces at the pump and
washstand outdoors, and combed back their hair.
Grandma and Aunt Inah welcomed them as they
entered the dining room and took their seats, polite
and a bit awkward. Grandpa offered thanks, and the

hungry men ate and drank first, so they could get back to work.

Women and children served them and got to eat after the men had vacated the chairs, and clean table service was laid down. Actually, this was a pleasant time of relaxation and enjoyment and fun for the women who had worked long and hard to prepare the delicious food and for Jay and me, who had done everything that was asked of us, too. There was always plenty of food for this "second sitting," and everyone enjoyed the time to rest and relax before we had to clear the table, clean up and wash and dry the dishes by hand in that extremely small kitchen, with not much counter space at all.

I don't think any of the women minded in the least that the men working out in those hot humid fields, among the ticks, chiggers and mosquitoes, breathing that air full of chaff and weed smells and dust, under the blazing sun, had sat down to eat first. They had to go right back to the fields with the hottest and most miserable part of the day ahead of them, and back at the farmhouse, we had our work to do, also. Both groups deserved a break, deserved some rest, some pleasure, some refreshment, liquid and nourishment for their bodies. As we ate, we talked about how much the men had enjoyed their food.

The women and children would be taking iced tea, lemonade and perhaps coffee, as well as cookies, sandwiches or some other light snack down to the fields for the three-thirty afternoon break. We did that for the mid-morning break, too.  Daddy or Aunt Inah usually drove a pickup truck to take the food and drink, and Jay and I might go along, to help serve the workers. Depending on the number of fields planted in grain and the size of the harvest, the work and the cooking might go on for at least two and sometimes three days.

Sometimes Grandpa or Uncle Paul told Jay and me to get into the back of the big farm truck into which the grain was pouring from the combine. This was a job I just adored.  We had to stay out of the way of the relentless fall of pungent grain, so as not to be smothered and buried alive.  Barefooted, we were supposed to keep the

Grandma feeding her chickens and a couple of holiday turkeys at her chicken house, with barn in the background.

fresh kernels from piling up in a huge mountain and spilling over the edges of the truck, using our hands, arms and legs to push the wheat, oats or rye toward the back of the truck bed as our bare feet sank in a delightful way down through the shifting sharply fragrant mass. Then we could have the pleasure of the same job when the grain was shoveled into large square bins the size of small rooms back in the barn.

I loved it, even if my skin broke out in a light rash and I had to have a cool soda bath before going to bed. I loved it in spite of the itchy red insect bites Mother would dab with Campho-Phenique or Calamine lotion while warning me not to scratch them. Removing the ticks without leaving their heads in my skin took far too long for sleepy me. Grandma and I were ready for bed on the sleeping porch.

After four or five days of hard work, and always after her duties were done, Grandma frequently took to her bed for a couple of days, suffering from a "sick" migraine headache. She would wrap a clean white rag tightly across her forehead. I'm afraid she did not get enough sympathy from the family, partly because nobody else had headaches like that and mostly because she had a characteristic pattern of moans and groans so loud they could be heard in every room of the house. Of course, I did not sleep with her when she was having a sick headache. Fortunately, she did not moan that way at night, only in the daytime.

# *Grandma's Gifts*

Grandma rarely gave Jay and me any kind of big physical or monetary gifts. She had been brought up in an extremely thrifty tradition. The lavishness of today and the showering of children with expensive gifts was unknown in her family. Of course, Jay and I were growing up in the Great Depression of the 1930s and World War II. Grandma never had money of her own except for "egg money" when she sold or traded excess eggs from her hens at the feed or grocery stores. One of her stock expressions was "I don't have any change."

Until Grandpa's original mortgage was paid off, money was tight at the farm and for all of us, in one way or another. There was always plenty of food, though, especially food that was grown and preserved by dent of hard work right on the farm.

At Christmas, we usually drew names. In years when we didn't, Grandma and Grandpa might give us a card containing two, three, four or five dollar bills, and the same for our birthdays. One of her favorite presents for me was a fine linen handkerchief, with lace, embroidery or cutwork. Today I love those handkerchiefs.

What Grandma gave Jay and me was herself and her time, the most priceless and precious gifts of all. She gave us fun and good food, gales of laughter and old time hymns. She was accepting and indulgent with us

Daddy and I are fishing in the pond closest to the farmhouse.

beyond measure, as she had never been with her own children. What she, Grandpa and other adults on the farm taught us was how to work hard, have fun while you were doing it and eat well on the fruits of your labor.

On rainy days when we were little, Grandma would let Jay and me put up a card table in the living room and drape a quilt or blanket over it to make a playhouse. We took our stuffed animals, especially the Winnie-the-Pooh ones, and my dolls inside. We had some black doll-sized wooden chairs and tables that Daddy had made for us, like the Three Bears might have used. We brought in little pots and pans and my second best play tea set. I remember taking a kitten inside with us a few times. I think we tied a bonnet under its chin, poor thing. But in a way, the kitten liked the attention for a while.

Sometimes we played Pick Up Sticks, Chinese Checkers, Old Maid, Rummy or Monopoly, and Grandma or any of the adults would sit down and play with us, if they had time. In fact, every one had more time to play with us on bad weather days.

We had a regular rubber tire swing under a tree and a sand pile in view of the front porch. We played there by the hour or in our clubhouse in the barn loft, which we swept clean and rearranged every summer, once it was empty of hay. This was our retreat where we could hatch up our plans and discuss what the adults had said and done and just what we thought of it. Before noonday dinner and supper, we asked Grandma and Aunt Inah what each was planning to serve, then decided where we would eat.

After I was grown and married, Grandma gave me two of her hooked rugs. She had very little design or color sense, but she knew how to cut old woolen garments into strips and use them to make hooked rugs. She left me wonderful handmade quilts passed down in her family and two silk and velvet comforter tops she had pieced from Mother's and my favorite dresses. Juanita had given her a set of a dozen footed crystal water goblets with three stripes of gold around the rims, which she always used for holiday dinners. One has a chip, but Grandma gave them to me, and I have always loved using them for special occasions, just as she did.

# The Last Half of Grandma's Life

Whenever we left to travel to the east or west coasts for a few months or a couple of years, Grandma would hang on the windows of the car with tears running down her face. "I'll probably not live long enough to ever see you again," she would wail in despair. She was in her forties and fifties in those days.

A few months after Grandpa died suddenly at the age of seventy-three, Grandma became ill, had some type of surgery and lingered near death for several months. She was so ill my aunt wanted to order provisions for out-of-town family and friends who might be coming in for Grandma's funeral, but my mother wouldn't let her. At the time, Grandma was in her late sixties. She recovered to live for almost thirty more years, alert and able to enjoy a good joke and a good laugh to the end. It makes me happy to know my children remember her well.

Grandma was baptized late in life, when she was at least eighty years old. She believed baptism by total immersion to be essential, but had procrastinated so long because she greatly feared going completely under water. Her oldest daughter helped her arrange to be privately baptized. Grandma felt happy about it afterward and told my mother it wasn't nearly as frightening as she thought it would be.

Shortly before she died at the age of ninety-five,

Grandma gave my mother a copy of this prayer, which she said had been her daily prayer every morning for a long time.

*God, go with me through this day.*
*Reveal each step along the way*
*that I may know Thy perfect plan*
*and all Thy wonders understand.*

*Give me the faith and strength I need*
*that I may know Thy will indeed.*
*Help me to feel Thy presence here*
*and know that Thou art always near.*

Mother handed Grandma's prayer down to me a few years ago, and now I love it, too, just as I love to remember everything about my Grandma Hammons.

January, 2006, SW Mo.

# *Roaring River Memories*

Even as children, we knew when we stepped into
the cool shade of the cavern and stared into
the bottomless spring gushing out from the earth
that the place was sacred, timeless and magical.

When I was a child, my parents and I sometimes came
here to cook breakfast, driving the sixty miles from
home to this long deep valley.  After a thrilling rapid
descent around S and hairpin curves when ears popped
and it seemed doubtful the brakes would hold, we drove
into Roaring River State Park, selected a spot by the
clear water tumbling over rock dams, and got out to
stretch our legs.

Daddy would build a campfire under a grate, and when
it died down a bit, Mother would lay cold bacon strips
side by side in her cast iron skillet and place it over the
fire.  She turned the bacon with a long-handled fork as it
sizzled.  Coffee came to a boil in a gray enamel ware
coffee pot with dark gray spots, its lid held on with  a
wire. The aroma of bacon and coffee filled the air.  I have
that coffee pot still.  We toasted bread on the grate or with
the fork. Mother fried tomato slices, too, red or green, and
then the eggs.  Sometimes she fried potatoes and onions.
We ate at a dark wooden picnic table.  How wonderful
everything tasted in the cool air!  Mother and Daddy
would both cast for trout in the rushing river.  If one was
caught, we cleaned, cooked and ate it on the spot.

The lodge and nearby hatchery were finished then,
as I recall, the cabins, picnic and campgrounds, dams,
steps, retaining walls and arched bridges, the work
completed in the 1930's by the CCC, the Civilian
Conservation Corps. Their outstanding rock work is
still beautiful today. It was only a year before my birth
and the stock market crash of 1929 when Thomas Sayman
bought twenty-four hundred acres surrounding the river
and gave it within a month to the state of Missouri. So
began Roaring River State Park. A thousand acres and
ten miles of hiking trails came later. More campgrounds,
a nature center, swimming pool and bathhouse.

I remember how much fun it was to walk on top of the stone edge of the long pools where Rainbow Trout were raised, how I held Daddy's or Mother's hand, looking down at the writhing dark fish. Each pool had a different size, from tiny minnows to foot long trout and longer, the ones ready to be released. The best part was climbing the stone steps by the small clear lake with its big clumps of moss and walking beside it along the path to Roaring River Spring. I remember watching for the huge fat trout swimming lazily in and out between the vivid floating moss. We called them lunkers. They were wily and old, the survivors.

Most of all, I remember following the curving path beside the lake, the sense of mystery and sudden drop in temperature as we approached the spring and stepped into the shadow of the overhanging bluff. It was not too far above our heads. The blue green color of the spring was mesmerizing. I stared and stared, entranced. We could see for some distance back into the cavern where the ceiling came closer and closer to the water. I wanted to go there in a boat. Mother held my hand even tighter. A walking trail led to Deer Leap on the steep stone bluff far above. A small waterfall came from even higher in the pines, cedars, oaks, dogwoods and redbuds.

My father lit a cigarette and leaned back against the bluff, taking in the scene. He read the sign aloud, "Average Flow: 20 Million Gallons of Water Daily." He took a drag on his cigarette and exhaled. "They say the Indians came here, too, going way back in time. They liked it as much as we do. They would camp here in the hottest months to fish and swim, grow some corn and beans, hide out from their enemies. During the Civil War, bushwhackers hid in these caves. When I was a boy, this valley became a fishing retreat."

My husband came to Roaring River with his parents, too, and later, we brought our children to the spring and the hatchery, where they walked along the stone edges and ran up and down the steep trails. We took up trout fishing and camping, first in a pup tent, then a small motor home, then a larger one. We took walks at night with our black Cocker Spaniel. Fishing at Roaring River became one of Elliott's favorite things to do. We learned we could catch trout only by using practically invisible two-pound test line with our spinning rods. Knots and snarls drove us batty. But we loved to eat the fresh trout broiled in lemon butter.

One by one, we brought our grandchildren to Roaring River and taught them to catch the unpredictable trout. I'll never forget blond Paul at age six, running up and down the banks with his first trout. "Grandma, Grandma, I caught one!" Once we celebrated Paul's birthday and a memorable Mother's Day at Roaring River with our two mothers in a cabin, us in our motor home and our daughter's family in their VW Camper nearby. Potluck dinner, birthday cake and all.

Second grandson Julian fell in love with fly fishing and refused to fish any other way.

Now we stay in the new Roaring River Inn and eat in the dining room. We celebrated New Year's Eve, 2000, there with our friends.  Last time Julian came from college in June to visit and fish, we stayed in one of the newly remodeled two-bedroom cabins.  He caught several fat trout on his fly rod and cooked three on our grill at home that night with his special lemon marinade.

Today the current is boiling out of the spring, a dark blue green, so deep for years no one could find the bottom. Divers would go down time and time again and finally found it at 224 feet.  A waterfall drips at a good rate in the large pool of the spring, hooded by pock-marked tan stone bluffs, while pigeons coo and fly back out of sight into the cavern that holds the spring.

June 5, 2002, SW Mo.

## At the Beach with Claire

Claire and Elliott play Gin Rummy.
Claire enjoys confusing her opponent by distraction.
She's eleven, our granddaughter,
a shrewd card player for years now.
She plays dumb, acts crazy, clowns around,
takes forever to play, disarms her hapless
adversaries in every way she can.
 "Do I have to throw away?" her grandfather asks.
"Yes, you do." She hums a little tune.
He knocks.  They add. "It looks like you won, Granddad."
One hundred and one is his total.  She writes it down.
"One hundred and one Dalmatians," she says.


"How do you make big cursive?" Claire asks.
She's watching me write a capitol J.  Her grandfather
and I don't quite understand her.  He thinks
she is saying, "How do you make big purses?"
When he understands she was saying, "How do you
make big cursive?" he quips back, "You've got to do a lot
of cussin'." Laughs and giggles all around.
She wants to know how to make a capitol J in cursive,
and I show her.  She practices. "My teacher doesn't want
us to write in cursive." she says.  "She wants us to print."
"I went to a school like that in Fifth and Sixth Grade,"
I tell her, "and had to go back to printing all the time,
after I had already learned cursive."
"After you'd already learned it?" she asks in amazement.

Claire clobbered me on her last game of Gin in a
hard fought contest of many hands. The score stood
at ninety for me and ninety six for Claire. When we
resumed play, I made an error in discarding and
failed to knock with six points remaining in my hand.
A couple of plays later, she ginned, knocked
and won the game. "That hand made me tense,"
I said. "It made me tense, too," she said.

I find a one-page story about food in *The New Yorker*
called "Sweet Memories" by Madhur Jaffrey and ask
Claire to read it to me. She reads it aloud quite well,
including the words *Sanskrit, om, Basmati rice, emulating*
and the names of Indian spices and fruits, such as
*coriander, cardamon, cumin, tamarinds* and *mangoes*, with
which she's far more familiar than most American girls
her age. There are a couple of words, whose meanings I
explain to her as best I can, but I am not sure of the
correct pronunciation of one of them.

Her grandfather and I are pleased and proud.
"You're a good reader, Claire," I say. "I can see we have
no need to worry about your reading from here on out."

Or her charm, strategy and card playing, either.


August 24, 2002
Tolovanna Inn, Tolovanna Park, Oreg.

## *Proposal Rock*

When we first saw Neskowin Beach in Oregon
we stayed three nights. A dramatic scene lay
beyond our window and sliding glass door.
Hawk Creek, newly down from the Coast Range,
flowed past our postage-stamp patio to merge with
Neskowin Creek. Together, they meandered
a few hundred yards through a broad expanse of sand
toward Proposal Rock. They mingled with the breaking
Pacific surf on either side of the huge haystack rock.

Proposal Rock is crowned with lush green growth of
Sitka spruce, hemlock, alder, short needle pine known

locally as bull pine, an undergrowth of broad-leafed
evergreens and garlanded with bright wild flowers.
I saw daisies, buttercups, tall Western dandelions far
more elegant and graceful than their Eastern cousins,
Queen Anne's lace, and, I believe, a type of milkweed.
Delightful shallow caverns with sandy floors indent the
base of the rock. Footpaths snake up through the trees.
The place must be a favorite site for romantic men in love
to ask the scary question and offer the engagement ring.
Thus its name, Proposal Rock.

The Pacific has its hazards here, as on all its shores.
At low tide in pleasant weather adults establish camps
with blankets, picnics, beach chairs and umbrellas, assist
in elaborate sand castle construction and keep watch
over children playing and splashing in the cold shallow
lakes of crystal waters formed by the two creeks in the
protected shelter of the great rock.

On either side is a broad beach. To the north, it stretches
as far as one can see. To the south, there is an ample
expanse of spacious beach between Proposal Rock and a
densely wooded headland that drops right into the
Pacific. Walking on that beach just south of the Rock
one day, we came upon mysterious pillars jutting up
from the sand and surf. From a distance, they looked
dark, nearly black. At first we thought they were the
remains of an old dock, pier or fence, but as we walked
around them and studied them, that possibility seemed
less and less likely. We could discern no pattern. The

pillars were not close enough together and were not arranged in an orderly fashion. When we came close enough to touch them, we found they would not move one bit. They were firmly rooted in the sand, but hard like stone and completely encrusted with barnacles, tiny blue mussels and other minuscule shellfish. The largest was a sea creature as tall as my shoulders, a beast emerging from the busy breaking waves, with an imposing head like a wild stallion or camel, tail flipped up high. Surely, one imagines, the pillars growing up from the sand came from deep in the earth, from its molten depths. Surely they are haystack rocks or mountains in the making. We speculated for a couple of days, then returned to examine and test them.

We learn the truth at last. The coastline was once fifty miles further west than it is now, and Neskowin was covered by a dense evergreen forest. The pillars are the remains of ancient tree trunks, broken off and buried in a cataclysmic earthquake. Volcanic eruptions may have occurred at the same time. Some scholars believe it happened two or three thousand years ago. Although these strange pillars or fingers occur up and down the Oregon coast, there are more at Neskowin than anywhere. Usually, they are seen only in winter. The summer of 2002 is the first one in memory in which so many have been exposed to view. The pillars are petrified wood, covered by barnacles. At Proposal Rock, we found on the beach, the remains of a petrified forest.

August 2002, Neskowin, Oreg.

## *Valentine's Day, 2-2002*
### *Palm Desert, California. For Elliott–*

In this desert oasis, we spend these February days
together reasserting ourselves as a couple,
together with no one else, these seventeen days
of the second year of the 21st Century,
celebrating our love and life together in this February
known in our families as the month of romance.

Each morning we drink tea, go down to breakfast,
swim and sun. We watch the Road Runners, Wrens,
Hummingbirds, golfers and a Jack rabbit from our
balcony. We eat pâté and crackers, sandwiches made
from Pumpernickel bread and drink a glass of
Gewurztraminer, followed by iced tea and fruit.

We read, take naps, play hard-fought games of Gin
Rummy and find our church on the corner of Portola.
We see some paintings, Joshua Trees, a few shows,
including *The Living Desert*, hear a string quartet, walk
among the ancient palms and along the stream bed of
Indian Canyons, dine on Chinese, French, Mexican and
Italian food, the last with glorious song. We follow the
Olympic Winter Games at Salt Lake City on TV.

We celebrate half a century and one more year of
marriage, half a century and two years as a couple,
sixty-eight years since we first knew each other.

Your father said today, the thirteenth, is the Potter
family's lucky day. It was the day he married your
mother, Friday, February thirteenth. My parents married
on the ninth and you and I on the fourth of February.

We have our red carnations, the ones you bought for me.
We have each other. We have these days together.
"These precious days I'll spend with you."* On our
wedding night, we heard Walter Huston sing the words.

*He sang "September Song" with music by Kurt Weill and lyrics
by Maxwell Anderson from the 1938 Broadway production
*Knickerbocker Holiday*, in which Huston appeared. We heard his
recording in the 1950 Hal B. Wallis film, *September Affair*.

# *Why and How I Write*

I write to convey my vision of the world, my ideas,
those lightning "Aha!" moments, my take on life.
I write to sort out my head, for therapy, to keep
my sanity. Sometimes I rapid-write whatever boils
to the surface, purple froth or green.

I write what I believe, what makes me mad,
I write about what upsets me, what I feel and what I see,
hoping for insight and wisdom, for inspiration,
the mysterious and divine creative touch.
I let it all boil up and out in my journals.
I'm not squeamish. I don't edit or censor until later,
until I get it all down on paper.

From my worries, I write, and from my obsessions,
from my enchantments and fantasies.
I dream my dreams, embroider and expand them 'til
they seem real and true. I can recall them and return
to those imaginary scenes and imaginary people.
I suspend my own disbelief, and my dreams take form
in stories, sometimes in poetry. In fiction, I write
what I think people will like to read. I entertain
and use all my skills, all the alchemy I know
to charm and fascinate the reader.

I let time go by, days, weeks, months or years.
Then I call on my inner critic, the left side of my brain,

the editor in me, get out my red pencil, read it again,
read it aloud. I take what could be good, usable,
presentable. I take what I need for the mill,
what's most universal, true and human. I sort,
delete, rewrite and polish. Maybe I call on someone I
trust for reactions. I check facts and spelling, put in and
take out commas, get out my dictionaries and reference
books. It's a tricky time when the heart and passion
can be completely removed.
"Am I making it better or making it worse?"
The computer both helps and hurts at this point.
I work, work, work (sometimes for years) to improve
what poured out of me from an unknown source.

The road leads to three forks: prose, fiction, poetry.
I've taken each path at times and will take all three again,
but the walk is vastly different on each path,
each branching lane and trail.

Next is the hardest part of all. Presentation, marketing,
proposals, writing outlines, the dreaded synopsis, the
cover letter. Submitting work. Going to workshops,
conferences, short courses, entering contests. Pitching
to agents and editors in two minutes. You try to be
yourself, but have to watch what you say at all times.
Just the opposite of the inspiration. You try to steel
yourself to be embraced and accepted or be rejected.
The latter happens most. Rejection never fails to hurt.

On the route of commercial prose, I worked twenty years

writing to sell products and promote. I enjoyed it and
got paid. Ditto for genre novels. I won a few prizes,
sold some meditations and poetry, judged local and
national contests. Enjoyed it all and learned from it, too.

One branch of the fiction lane combines with poetry
to produce the drama route, an intriguing road I've not
yet traveled. It subdivides many times into stage and
screen plays for theater, TV, radio and film, books and
lyrics for musical productions, both classical and popular.

I write because I like to, in all kinds of ways, for
all kinds of reasons, but sometimes I wonder why I do.

Keep your day job. It isn't an easy walk.
It's addicting. You'll never be bored
or ever lack for opportunity to work at your craft.

Rewards are elusive, fleeting and mostly intangible.                    .

With thanks to Gabriele Lusser Rico, *Writing the Natural Way,*
Henriette Anne Klauser, *Writing on both Sides of the Brain,* Natalie
Goldberg, *Writing Down the Bones* and *Wild Mind,* Heather Hughes-
Calero, Writing *as a Tool for Self-Discovery,* and Dr. Joy Dworkin,
now Professor of English, Missouri Southern State Univ., Joplin, Mo.

Visit www.jacquelinepotter.com for more information and news.

Jacqueline Potter welcomes comments and reactions from readers, artists, those embarked on finding and walking their spiritual paths, writers, nature lovers and reading groups. (See Discussion Guide for Reading Groups on Page 183 of this book.)

To order additional copies of *By Surf and By Stream, New and Collected Poems and Reflections* by Jacqueline Potter, ask your local book dealer, order from your favorite internet bookstore, go to www.jacquelinepotter.com, or contact Living Water Press directly by e-mail or fax, if possible. Otherwise, use postal service or phone.

LIVING WATER PRESS
Att: Jean Riley
P.O. Box 567
Carthage, MO 64836-0567
Fax: 417-359-8494
E-mail: livingwaterpress@sbcglobal.net or
         livingwaterpress@joplin.com

Telephone: (417) 359-8308 or (417) 850-0637.

For information regarding special discounts for bulk purchases, please contact livingwaterpress@sbcglobal.net or livingwaterpress@joplin.com, Att: Jean Riley.

# Taste My Grandma's Delicious Recipes.

## Grandma's Spanish Roast

2 ½ to 6 ½ lb. beef roast (chuck, arm, rump or other)
Remove excess fat before cooking, if desired.

| | |
|---|---|
| 1 quart canned tomatoes | 1 teaspoon cinnamon |
| 1 large onion chopped fine | 1 teaspoon allspice |
| ½ cup vinegar | Salt to taste |
| ½ cup sugar | |

Boil meat tender with tomatoes, onion, vinegar, sugar and spices in covered Dutch oven or large heavy covered saucepan. Bring to a boil, then cover and turn temperature down to low or medium low so liquids are just simmering for at least 2-4 hours until meat is fork tender. Remove cover during last 30 minutes of cooking and watch closely, stirring occasionally. Simmer down low until sauce is thick. Taste for salt and seasoning. Beef should be extremely tender. Top meat with sauce or serve sauce in a bowl on the side.

## Grandma's Old-Fashioned Salad Dressing

| | |
|---|---|
| ½ cup vinegar | Salt and pepper to taste |
| 3/4 cup sugar | 2 eggs, beaten in bowl |
| Butter, the size of a walnut | ½ cup cream |
| 1 teaspoon prepared mustard | |

In a medium saucepan, put vinegar, sugar, butter, mustard, salt and pepper on to cook and bring to a boil. Pour hot mixture over beaten eggs in small mixing bowl, stirring rapidly as you pour. Return mixture to saucepan over medium low to medium heat, then let come to a boil, stirring all the while. Remove from burner and allow to cool, then stir in ½ cup of cream, either whipping cream, half and half or evaporated milk. May use at once or store in refrigerator in glass jar with a tight-fitting lid. Will keep in refrigerator for two to four weeks. This dressing is delicious on chunked head lettuce, with or without fresh tomatoes. It is also good on shredded Napa Chinese cabbage, served in small dishes.

## Grandma's Cherry Pudding-Cake

**Batter**

1 cup sugar

2 teaspoons baking powder

Pinch of salt

Butter, size of egg, melted or softened

Flour to make a stiff batter, 1 3/4-2 cups

1 cup milk

**Cherry Filling**

1 ½ cups red cherries, fresh, frozen or canned     1 cup sugar

Small pieces of butter     2 cups boiling water

Preheat oven to 375º. Mix cup of sugar with baking powder and salt. Work in butter. Add flour, then milk, beating in with spoon. Pour into a greased 12 ½" x 7 ½" baking dish or pan. For filling, sweeten cherries as desired, add butter, boiling water, stir once and pour on top of batter. Bake about 45 minutes. Serve warm if possible, with milk, cream, whipped cream or vanilla ice cream.

## Grandma's Cold Pressed Chicken

1 bone-in whole chicken, capon or rooster with skin, 3.5 to 6.5 lbs., may be cut into parts     Salt and pepper to taste

Part of a medium sweet onion to taste, scraped or ground with chicken, if desired     I like pepper and some onion.

Boil a 3.5 to 6.5 lb. fowl or two small ones at low temperature until tender, adding salt to taste. Cool, then transfer cooked chicken to large plate. Cook liquid down to a rich broth as you remove meat from skin and bones. Grind boneless chicken in meat grinder or food processor, also grinding in a little raw sweet onion, to taste, if desired. Chicken should be chopped fine, not pulverized. Place ground chicken and onion in bowl or 9"x5" loaf pan or dish, with enough chicken broth to moisten ground chicken, but not so much as to leave broth standing on top. Taste and adjust seasonings. Cover and chill for several hours or overnight in the refrigerator until congealed. Slice congealed pressed chicken and remove slices carefully with small spatula or pie server. Serve at once on leaf lettuce on chilled plate or platter or in sandwiches. Keep cool or cold.

## Grandma's Wilted Lettuce

1-10 slices of bacon
Reserved bacon drippings
Apple cider vinegar to taste
Hot water, if needed
Salt and ground pepper

Fresh soft leaf lettuce, adjust
 quantity for # of servings
Fresh green onions
Fresh red radishes
Bit of sugar if desired, to taste

Use soft types of extremely fresh lettuce, such as leaf lettuce, Bibb, Boston or Buttercrunch lettuce. Radishes and green onions should be tasty. This salad can wilt down to half its volume if dressing is hot enough. Fry bacon until crisp in skillet. Remove and drain. Reserve some bacon fat in skillet. Wash leaf lettuce, drain and tear or cut into very large pottery or glass bowl. Slice or chop green onions and red radishes, adding to leaf lettuce in bowl. Break up crisp bacon and sprinkle on top of salad with freshly ground black pepper. Heat desired amount of bacon drippings in skillet. (I do not like my wilted lettuce too greasy.) Add 2 tablespoons vinegar and a bit of sugar, if desired. Keep warm. Just before serving, add a little water and vinegar to taste, bring to boil. Sprinkle salad with salt, pour hot liquid on top, toss, adjust seasonings, serve.

## Grandma's Pumpkin Pie

1 cup sugar
1 heaping tablespoon flour
1/4 teaspoon salt
1/4 teaspoon ground cloves
1/4 teaspoon allspice

1/4 teaspoon ginger
½ teaspoon cinnamon
1 cup canned pumpkin
1 egg
1 ½ cups milk

This will fill one 9" or 10" unbaked pie shell. Preheat oven to 400°. Combine dry ingredients. Place pumpkin in mixing bowl. Beat in egg, then milk until well mixed. Add dry ingredients and beat again until smooth. Pour into unbaked pie shell and place on bottom rack of preheated 400° oven. After ten minutes, reduce temperature to 325° and bake until crust is light gold and filling is completely set. If edges start to brown, lay piece of aluminum foil over pie. Table knife blade in center should come out clean. Serve with whipped cream.

## Grandma's Potato Cakes

2 cups stiff mashed potatoes, seasoned to taste      1 egg
Butter, lard, margarine or vegetable oil      Flour

Put flour on plate or waxed paper. Break egg into cold mashed potatoes and work with fork or fingers until thoroughly mixed. Divide into rough balls, then shape and flatten into patties 2 to 2 ½ inches across, smoothing the edges. Place each pattie on flour and turn once to dredge. Heat shortening or oil in skillet over medium heat. Using spatula, carefully transfer potato cakes into medium-hot fat. Fry until golden brown on each side, turning once. Take up on plate and serve immediately.

## Grandma's Cornmeal Mush and Fried Slices

1 cup cornmeal, white or yellow      4 cups water
1 teaspoon salt or to taste

Bring 3 cups of water to a boil. Combine remaining 1 cup of water, cornmeal and salt. Slowly pour into boiling water, stirring constantly. Lower heat and cook until thickened, stirring frequently. Cover and continue cooking over low heat 5 minutes. Stir. Remove from heat but keep warm and serve hot. Similar to grits, cornmeal mush may be eaten with butter or margarine and syrup, if desired, or in a bowl with milk, cream and sugar or other sweetening. Makes 8-10 servings.

Grandma always made enough to pour leftover cornmeal mush into a rectangular glass or metal loaf pan and chill overnight in the ice box or refrigerator. Sometimes she would mix in crumbled cooked bacon or pork cracklings. Next morning, she sliced the cold mush into even slices, about 1/4" to 3/8" thick and fried them golden brown in hot fat, butter or other shortening. She served them with syrup, sorghum molasses or honey. They were simply delicious with eggs and breakfast meats.

## Grandma's Fried Apples

Several cooking apples                              Sugar
Butter, shortening, fat and/or vegetable oil

Cut apples in quarters, core and slice into wedges about ½"
thick, enough to fill your skillet heaping full. Heat to medium
in non-stick skillet with cover, a generous amount of any
combination of butter, lard, bacon grease, margarine,
shortening or vegetable oil. When melted, add apple slices.
Watch carefully, lower heat and turn often with spatula, for
they burn easily. They will cook down. Cover, but continue
turning often. When done, sprinkle with sugar to taste. Allow
to melt, turn, taste, add more sugar if desired, but be more
careful than ever now to watch and turn, as they will burn
more easily than before. Remove from heat, cover and serve as
soon as possible.

## Grandma's Baked Apples

Baking apples, 1 for each serving, Rome apples a good choice
For 6 apples, 3/4 cup plus 2 T sugar  Water  Raisins, if desired

Preheat oven to 350 degrees F. Wash apples and remove cores
from centers using small paring knife or apple corer. Starting
at stem end, peel apples about 1/3 of way down. Arrange in
shallow baking pan, pared side up. Boil 3/4 cup sugar with 1
cup of water and some apple peel for 10 minutes, stirring and
lowering heat once it comes to a boil. Remove from heat.
Remove peel. Grandma usually filled each apple with a few
raisins. Pour sugar syrup slowly over apples, so each apple is
bathed in syrup and core holes are filled. Place on lower rack
of oven to bake ½ to 1 hour until easily pierced with fork.
Spoon syrup from pan over apples frequently. When tender,
remove pan from oven. Baste all with syrup. Sprinkle top of
each apple with 1 teaspoon sugar. Broil under low heat,
basting often, until brown. Watch carefully as apples will burn
easily. Serve warm or cool, with cream or milk, if desired.

# *Discussion Guide for Reading Groups*

1. How does the author view and describe the creative process and its relationship to inspiration as she has experienced it?

2. Does the author paint a character portrait of anyone? If so, who?

3. Direct the group's attention to a phrase, poem or part of the book that speaks to you.

4. Have you experienced any of the author's thoughts, reactions and feelings?

5. How do you react to the pen-and-ink drawings and the old black-and-white photographs in "Spring River Saga"? Which ones do you especially like?

6. *By Surf and By Stream* is a decidedly personal book. Is it too personal for you? What do you learn about the author and what extra dimension does the collection gain because she has included the dates and places where the poems and reflections were written and has also included the "Early Poems" and "Spring River Saga"?

7. Point out specific poems or reflections about everyday life, people, especially family and friends, aspects of nature and what they mean to the author, and any of her beliefs, faith and attitudes toward living you would like to comment upon, question or discuss.

# How This Book Came to Be

Jacqueline Potter has been writing poetry since she was "hooked" in third grade at P.S. 101, Forest Hills, Long Island, N.Y. Her family had just moved there from Kansas City. The next year they moved to New York City's Upper West Side, and all spent summers with her grandparents on their Southwest Missouri farm.

"My love affair with the seashore began on the east coast," she says, "and only intensified when I lived in Long Beach, California, and the San Francisco Bay area. That love affair goes on, no matter where I live.

"Since most of my income as an adult has come from other forms of writing, first advertising and public relations, then from publication of my two novels, I've never thought of myself primarily as a poet. I have always written poetry when it suddenly came to me, when it boiled up inside me, or for the pure joy of it.

"When I began to gather these poems together, I asked my artist husband to illustrate them with a few pen-and-ink drawings. At first, he grumbled that he had far more pressing things to do, but as he worked, a happy smile appeared upon his face.

"I kept polishing older poems and writing many new ones, adding a section of recollections close to my heart called "Spring River Saga", with thirty-three old photos and my grandmother's recipes. My husband kept improving his drawings and making new pen-and-ink illustrations. When the book was nearly done, I suddenly realized this collection tells exactly who I am and what I believe in, and tells it more truly than any other form of writing could possibly do.

"Somehow, the collection had become poetry as personal history, as self-portrait, as memoir. Just by being put together, the poems and reflections became a testament to all that is precious to me, especially my relationships to family and friends and to nature itself."